CAKE DECORATING

The Complete Step-by-Step Guide

CAKE DECORATING

The Complete Step-by-Step Guide

Carol Deacon

NEW
HOLLAND

DEDICATION
In memory of Malcolm Martin Deacon who loved
fishing, cricket...and cake!

First published in paperback in 2005 by
New Holland Publishers (UK) Ltd
London • Cape Town • Sydney • Auckland

Garfield House
86–88 Edgware Road
London W2 2EA
www.newhollandpublishers.com

80 McKenzie Street
Cape Town 8001
South Africa

Level 1, Unit 4
14 Aquatic Drive
Frenchs Forest, NSW 2086
Australia

218 Lake Road
Northcote, Auckland
New Zealand

3 5 7 9 10 8 6 4 2

ISBN 1 84537 186 0

Senior Editor: Clare Hubbard
Designer: Isobel Gillan
Photographer: Shona Wood
Additional photography: Edward Allwright and Chris Turner
Additional steps and cake shots: Janice Murfitt
Editorial Direction: Rosemary Wilkinson
Production: Hazel Kirkman

Reproduction by Modern Age Repro House Ltd, Hong Kong
Printed and bound in Malaysia by Times Offset (M) sdn Bhd

NOTES
Every effort has been made to present clear and accurate instructions. Therefore, the author
and publishers can offer no guarantee or accept any liability for any injury, illness or damage
which may inadvertently be caused to the user while following these instructions.

Because of the slight risk of salmonella, raw eggs should not be served to the
very young, the ill or elderly, or to pregnant women.

In the recipes use either metric or imperial measurements, but never a combination of
the two, as exact conversions are not always possible.

ACKNOWLEDGEMENTS
Carol Deacon would like to thank Pamela Eve, Elyane, Paul, Stephen, Rosie and Holly Jones
and Juliette and Charlie for their help "Twiggy sitting" during the making of this book. Carol
would also like to thank Valerie Hedgethorne for her marzipan recipe on page 84.

The cake shown on page 2 is the Wedding star (see pages 104–105).

CONTENTS

INTRODUCTION 6

BAKING BASICS 8

CAKE RECIPES 10

NUMBER AND LETTER
CAKES 16

BASIC EQUIPMENT 22

BUTTERCREAM ICING 26

Techniques 26

Cakes 32

SUGARPASTE 60

Techniques 60

Cakes 68

MARZIPAN 84

ROYAL ICING 90

Techniques 90

Cakes 102

CHOCOLATE 114

Techniques 114

Cakes 120

Suppliers 140

Index 143

INTRODUCTION

Probably the most commonly uttered phrase when a decorated cake is brought out at a celebration is "Oh isn't that lovely...", quickly followed by "I could never do that!" Well, guess what? Neither could I, once.

The secret behind successful cake decorating is not having a steady hand, an eye for colour, a creative mother or any of the other excuses that I've heard over the years. In fact, there are really only two secrets. The first is – to have a go and the second – allow yourself enough time.

However, just launching yourself up the home baking aisle in the supermarket or into your nearest cake decorating equipment stockist with no real idea of what to buy will result in bewilderment, frustration and, quite possibly, an empty space on the table where a cake should be. So here's how the *Complete Step-by-Step Guide to Cake Decorating* can help you.

From baking the perfect sponge through to icing a wedding cake, I have explained and demystified many of the techniques used, to create simple but stunning cakes. This is not the most technical cake book on the market but that's because I have tried to take the simplest route to a great end result without scaring anyone!

Primarily this book is aimed at the beginner or those with a little experience who want to take their skills further. However, because some of the ideas are so simple and quick, it will also appeal to those with years of experience too. After all, you may be the most experienced cake decorator in the world but I bet you still get asked to produce things at the last minute!

It is easy to forget that cooking, especially preparing special items like this, is not knowledge that any of us is born with. It involves reading, learning and practice. However, I believe that learning should be enjoyable, information understandable and great results easily attainable.

So, now you are about to learn a lot of new things that you never knew you wanted to know. But best of all, you are about to bring joy to a lot of people. Just watch their faces light up when you bring out your creation and I bet if you listen carefully you'll hear the odd whisper of "Oh isn't that lovely...I could never do that!"

Carol Deacen

RIGHT *Easter cake, see page 124.*

BAKING BASICS

This section gives you all of the basic information that you need to know before you actually start making the cake. There is advice on what you need to think about before you start, cake sizes and portions, information on baking tins and how to line them and a fail-safe way of calculating how much mixture you need. Basically, you'll find everything you need to know to get you started.

There are certain questions that you need to think about beforehand to ensure that the finished cake is everything that you wanted it to be:

* ✶ How many people will the cake need to serve?
* ✶ What sort of cake does/do the recipient/s like?
* ✶ What style of cake is needed?
* ✶ How much time have you got?
* ✶ Are there things you can do in advance?

Cake sizes and portions

To get the maximum number of portions out of a cake, it is best to cut it into fingers rather than wedges.

To give you an idea of the size of cake you should be baking, opposite is a guide to the approximate number of portions you can get from cakes of various sizes.

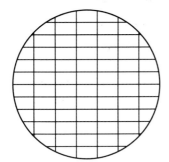 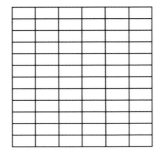

ABOVE *These diagrams show the best way to cut a round and a square cake.*

Cutting cakes

To be sure you have enough to feed everyone, a cutting cake can be made. This cake does not have any decoration on it. It should be made to match the main cake – fruit, sponge, chocolate or whatever and covered with the same kind of icing, but it is then left plain, as it will never be on show. It is especially useful at weddings to have a spare cake like this to provide lots of extra slices.

SIZE AND PORTION GUIDE		
	Sponge Cake	Fruit Cake
15cm (6in) round	10	20
15cm (6in) square	15	25
18cm (7in) round	15	30
18cm (7in) square	20	40
20cm (8in) round	20	40
20cm (8in) square	25	50
23cm (9in) round	25	50
23cm (9in) square	35	70
25cm (10in) round	30	65
25cm (10in) square	45	90
28cm (11in) round	40	85
28cm (11in) square	55	110
30cm (12in) round	50	100
30cm (12in) square	65	130

Baking tins

There are all sorts of tins available for baking cakes. Some are rigid all-in-one tins, others have a spring-release mechanism that releases the sides of the tin, freeing the cake and others have a separate top and side section that allows you to push the cake out of the tin when baked. There is also an increasing range of shaped tins available, from numbers and letters, hearts and stars, to cartoon characters. There is no hard and fast rule as to what type of tin (spring-release, rigid etc.) is best for a particular cake. You just need to ensure that whatever size or shape of tin you use will provide you with enough cake for your chosen design.

Lining a cake tin

Lining a cake tin sometimes seems like the most tedious part of the whole cake-making process, but it really is the only way to ensure that all of your cake comes out of the tin in one piece. There are a couple of new products on the market, "cake sprays" that claim that if you use them there is no need to line your tin. I can't comment on whether they are effective or not as I've never used them, I prefer to line my tins.

Some kitchen and specialist stores sell paper cake tin liners which you simply put in the tin with no need to add grease of any sort. One has been used in the Monster chocolate cup cake on page 132 and even becomes part of the finished creation.

You can use either greaseproof paper or baking parchment to line the tin. The only difference is that the baking parchment does not need to be greased.

1 Measure the circumference and height of the tin. Cut out a strip of greaseproof paper or baking parchment to that length and about 2cm (1in) wider than the height of the tin.

2 Place the tin onto another piece of paper or parchment and draw around the base. Cut out the drawn shape.

3 Wipe a little butter or margarine around the inside of the tin.

4 Place the long strip around the inside of the tin (Fig. a). Slip the other piece into the bottom of the tin.

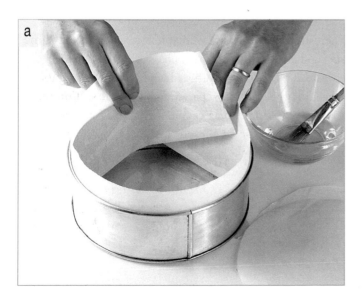

Lining a cake tin for fruit cake

The method for lining a tin ready for baking a fruit cake is exactly the same as for a sponge cake, except that you need to double line the tin. This protects the sides and base of the cake during its long cooking time. So cut out two strips for the sides and two base pieces.

It is also advisable to wrap a double layer of brown or greaseproof paper around the outside of the tin. Tie string around the outside to hold it in place (Fig. b).

How to calculate how much mixture is needed for an unusual shaped tin

Not all cake tins are square or round. Here's a handy tip to work out how much cake mixture you need.

1 Fill a cup with water. Tip the water into the tin. Repeat until the water has reached the level that the unbaked cake mixture would reach if the tin were filled. Usually about 2.5cm (1in) from the top. Count the cupfuls.

2 Now take a cake tin for which you know how much cake mixture would be needed. For instance, a 20-cm (8-in) round tin which would take a four-egg sponge mixture. Using the same cup, count how many cupfuls of water would be needed to fill that tin.

3 If the number of cupfuls to fill the unusual shaped tin is double the cupfuls required to fill the 20-cm (8-in) round tin, then you know that you need to make double the quantity of cake mixture. If it is half then you know to you need to make half and so on.

CAKE RECIPES

In the rush to get to the exciting, decorating part, it is easy to overlook the baking. However, no matter how exotic the cake looks, a cake is made to be eaten and it absolutely has to taste as good as it looks. Here are some basic cake recipes which are my reliable favourites and they always taste great.

Madeira sponge

This sponge cake recipe is extremely easy. You just put all the ingredients in a bowl and mix. A food mixer makes light work of the mixing and takes only a minute. It will take longer if you're mixing by hand. To make things easier for yourself, make sure the butter is very soft.

INGREDIENTS				
SQUARE TIN		15cm (6in)	18cm (7in)	20cm (8in)
ROUND TIN	15cm (6in)	18cm (7in)	20cm (8in)	23cm (9in)
Self-raising flour	175g (6oz)	225g (8oz)	285g (10oz)	350g (12oz)
Caster sugar	115g (4oz)	170g (6oz)	230g (8oz)	285g (10oz)
Butter (softened)	115g (4oz)	170g (6oz)	230g (8oz)	285g (10oz)
Eggs (medium)	2	3	4	5
Milk	15ml (1 tbsp)	15ml (1 tbsp)	30ml (2 tbsp)	45ml (3 tbsp)
Baking time (approx)	1¼–1½hrs	1¼–1½hrs	1½–1¾ hrs	1½–2 hrs

1 Grease and line the relevant cake tin (see page 8) and preheat your oven to 150°C/300°F/Gas mark 2. (Timings and temperatures for fan-assisted ovens may vary. Refer to your manufacturer's handbook for guidance.)

2 Sift the flour into a mixing bowl to get some air into it and add all the rest of the ingredients.

3 Set the mixer to a slow setting and slowly bind all of the ingredients together.

4 Increase the speed and beat for a minute until the mixture has become pale and silky.

5 Spoon the mixture into a prepared tin and smooth the top.

6 Bake for the required time. When ready, the cake should have pulled away slightly from the edges of the tin. If pressed lightly, the top should spring back from the touch. Insert a sharp knife or cake skewer into the cake. If it comes out clean, the cake is ready.

7 Turn the cake out of the tin, upside down onto a cooling rack. Peel off the lining and leave to cool.

STORING: Ice cake when cool or wrap in clingfilm until ready. Use and eat within five days.
FREEZING: Once baked and cooled, this sponge can be frozen for up to three months.

Flavour variations

CHOCOLATE Add a tablespoon of cocoa powder in place of a tablespoon of flour for a quick chocolate sponge.
ORANGE/LEMON For a hint of citrus, add the grated zest of an orange or lemon before baking.
ALMOND Add a teaspoon of essence to the basic mixture.
COCONUT Add 60g (2oz) desiccated coconut to the mixture.

Pudding bowl, sandwich and fairy cakes

Use the three-egg sponge mixture to make a 1-litre (2-pint) pudding bowl cake for the Monster cup cake (see page 132), 24 fairy cakes for the Fearsome dragon (see page 70) or two sandwich cakes for the Quick chocolate cake on page 120.

Make sure the pudding bowl is heatproof. Grease the inside and place a disc of greaseproof paper in the base. When the cake is cooked, slide a palette knife around the edge of the bowl to release it. Tip onto a cooling rack and peel off the greaseproof disc. If you don't have a bowl, bake a round cake and carve it into a rounded shape.

RIGHT *Fairy cakes are fun, easy to make and can be decorated in many different ways.*

Chocolate cake

This cake takes a little more effort than the simple chocolate sponge recipe on page 10, but the velvet texture of the finished cake makes the trouble worthwhile. A crust will form on the top of the cake as it cooks, it might even scorch slightly. Don't worry, this is normal and will not affect the taste of the cake underneath. Slice the crust off the cake after it has cooled and just before decorating.

INGREDIENTS				
SQUARE TIN		15cm (6in)	18cm (7in)	20cm (8in)
ROUND TIN	15cm (6in)	18cm (7in)	20cm (8in)	23cm (9in)
Butter (softened)	90g (3oz)	115g (4oz)	170g (6oz)	230g (8oz)
Caster sugar	40g (1¼oz)	75g (2½oz)	115g (4oz)	150g (5oz)
Eggs (medium)	3	4	6	8
Plain chocolate	150g (5oz)	170g (6oz)	230g (8oz)	285g (10oz)
Self-raising flour	90g (3oz)	115g (4oz)	170g (6oz)	230g (8oz)
Icing sugar	30g (1oz)	30g (1oz)	60g (2oz)	90g (3oz)
Baking time (approx)	45–55 mins	45mins–1 hr	1–1¼ hrs	1–1¼ hrs

1 Grease and line the relevant cake tin (see pages 8–9) and preheat the oven to 180°C/350°F/Gas mark 4. (Timings and temperatures for fan-assisted ovens may vary. Refer to your manufacturer's handbook for guidance.)

2 Separate the egg whites from the yolks and set aside in two small bowls.

3 Melt the chocolate in a heatproof bowl (see page 114).

4 In a mixing bowl, cream the softened butter and caster sugar together.

5 Beat in the egg yolks and then the melted chocolate.

6 Set the mixer to a low speed and slowly stir in the flour. Stop as soon as it has all been incorporated. Set aside.

7 Put the egg whites into a second mixing bowl. Connect the whisk attachment to your mixer and whisk the egg whites until stiff. Whisk in the icing sugar.

8 Re-attach the beater to the mixer and slowly stir the chocolate mixture into the egg whites.

9 Pour into a prepared tin and bake immediately. The crust on top of the cake can make it difficult to tell if the cake is cooked by touch alone so carefully cut a little section of crust away from the centre of the cake. Insert a knife or cake skewer. If it comes out clean, the cake is ready.

10 Turn the cake out onto a cooling rack. Remove the greaseproof paper and leave to cool.

STORING: Ice within a day of baking. If this is not possible, freeze until required.
FREEZING: When cooled, this cake will freeze well for up to three months. Leave the crust on if freezing.

LEFT *Quick chocolate cake (see page 120).*

Special effects with sponge cake

Forget decorating for a moment, there are a few special effects that can be achieved with the cake itself.

Chequered sponge

This effect is fun, as from the outside it looks like an ordinary cake, but when you cut into it you have a chequered effect. You need two round sponge cakes of contrasting colours; usually a plain sponge and a chocolate sponge are used.

1 Using cutters, cut two rounds out of the plain sponge. Do the same with the chocolate cake (Fig. a).

2 Before assembling the cake, coat the inside of each piece with buttercream or jam. Swap the middles around – so the middle of the chocolate cake goes into the middle of the plain sponge and vice versa (Fig. b).

3 Sandwich the cakes together with your chosen filling (Fig. c).

Stripy sponge

This is another way of adding interest to the cake itself. Children particularly like the surprise of seeing the unexpected when the cake is cut. You need two round sponge cakes of contrasting colours; usually a plain sponge and a chocolate sponge are used.

1 Cut each cake in half. Reassemble the cake by sandwiching together the plain and chocolate sponge pieces in alternate layers (Fig. d).

2 You can use your filling of choice to assemble the layers. Try to keep the layers as level as possible (Fig. e).

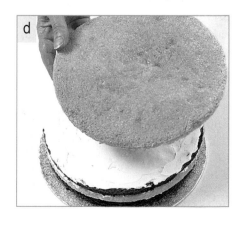

Fruit cake

I've said this before, but I'll say it again as it's so true – there is absolutely nothing to beat the seasonal aroma of cinnamon and spices wafting through the house in the dreary winter months before Christmas. Visitors to your home will not only want to stir the mixture and make a wish, but they'll start telling you tales of how they used to visit their grannies when they were young, how she used to bake wonderful cakes and before you know it, you will have spread Christmas spirit without even trying.

Making your own fruit cake is a lot easier than you might think. The secret is to make sure you've got everything together before you start.

INGREDIENTS				
SQUARE TIN	15cm (6in)	18cm (7in)	20cm (8in)	23cm (9in)
ROUND TIN	18cm (7in)	20cm (8in)	23cm (9in)	25cm (10in)
Currants	150g (5oz)	175g (6oz)	200g (7oz)	225g (8oz)
Raisins	150g (5oz)	175g (6oz)	200g (7oz)	225g (8oz)
Sultanas	150g (5oz)	175g (6oz)	200g (7oz)	225g (8oz)
Mixed peel	30g (1oz)	45g (1½oz)	60g (2oz)	75g (2½oz)
Glacé cherries	60g (2oz)	75g (2½oz)	90g (3oz)	100g (3½oz)
Brandy	60ml (4tbsp)	90ml (6tbsp)	120ml (8tbsp)	120ml (8tbsp)
Butter(softened)	150g (5oz)	175g (6oz)	200g (7oz)	225g (8oz)
Sugar (soft, dark brown)	150g (5oz)	175g (6oz)	200g (7oz)	225g (8oz)
Eggs (medium)	3	4	5	6
Plain flour	175g (6oz)	200g (7oz)	225g (8oz)	270g (9oz)
Mixed spice	2 tsp	2 tsp	1 tbsp	1 tbsp
Cinnamon	½ tsp	½ tsp	¾ tsp	1 tsp
Lemon (zest only)	½	½	1	1
Ground almonds	20g (¾oz)	30g (1oz)	45g (1½oz)	60g (2oz)
Flaked almonds	20g (¾oz)	30g (1oz)	45g (1½oz)	60g (2oz)
Baking time (approx)	1½–2 hrs	1¾–2¼ hrs	2–2¼ hrs	2¼–2¾ hrs

1 Place all the dried fruits into a bowl and pour the brandy over them. Stir and cover the bowl with a plate. Leave the fruits to soak for a few hours, preferably overnight.

2 Prepare the cake tin (see page 9) and preheat the oven to 150°C/300°F/Gas mark 2. (Timings and temperatures for fan-assisted ovens may vary. Refer to your manufacturer's handbook for guidance.)

3 Cream the butter and sugar together, then beat in the eggs.

4 Slowly mix in the sifted flour, spices and ground almonds. Add a little more flour if it seems too runny.

5 Stir in the soaked fruits, lemon zest and flaked almonds. Spoon the mixture into the prepared tin. Smooth the surface and bake.

6 Check the cake 15–20 minutes before the end of the baking time. If the top is turning very brown, place a disc of greaseproof paper over the top.

7 To test the cake, insert a sharp knife or cake skewer. If it comes out clean, the cake is done.

8 Allow the cake to cool completely in the tin. If using the cake straightaway, turn it out of the tin when cooled and remove the paper.

STORING: You can store this cake for up to three months. When cooled, tip it out of the baking tin and leave the greaseproof paper around the sides. Poke a few holes in the top of the cake with a cocktail stick and drizzle over some brandy. Let the brandy soak in and then wrap the cake in two sheets of greaseproof paper. Double wrap it again using two sheets of aluminium foil and place in a box or cupboard until required. Do not store it in a plastic airtight container as this can encourage mould growth. You can "feed" your cake every one to two weeks with a little more brandy if you wish.

FREEZING: If you plan to keep the cake longer than three months, wrap in greaseproof paper and freeze until required. Defrost throughly for about 8 hours at room temperature.

Microwave cakes

In case of emergency, here are a couple of cakes you can cook in four minutes! The texture is slightly different to that of oven-baked cakes and the vanilla cake will look pale as it will not brown on the top. Never use a metal cake tin in a microwave oven.

Vanilla cake

This recipe is for an 18-cm (7-in) round microwave cake dish or a l-litre (2-pint) microwave-safe pudding bowl.

120g (4oz) butter
120g (4oz) caster sugar
2 eggs
1 tsp vanilla essence
120g (4oz) self-raising flour
½ tsp baking powder

1 Grease the microwave dish/bowl and place a disc of greaseproof paper in the base.

2 Cream the butter and sugar together until fluffy. Beat in the eggs and vanilla essence. Fold in the flour and baking powder.

3 Spoon into the prepared dish and bake on full power for four minutes (or until a cocktail stick inserted in the centre of the cake comes out clean).

4 Leave the cake to stand for 10 minutes before turning out onto a cooling rack.

Chocolate cake

This recipe is for an 18-cm (7-in) round microwave cake dish or a l-litre (2-pint) microwave-safe pudding bowl.

120g (4oz) butter
120g (4oz) caster sugar
2 eggs
90g (3oz) self-raising flour
30g (1oz) cocoa powder
1 tsp baking powder

1 Grease the microwave dish/bowl and place a disc of greaseproof paper in the base.

2 Cream the butter and sugar together until fluffy.

3 Beat in the eggs. Stir in the flour, cocoa and baking powder.

4 Cook on full power for four minutes (or until a cocktail stick inserted in the centre comes out clean).

5 Leave the cake to stand for 10 minutes before turning out on to a cooling rack.

Troubleshooting

We all want our cakes to turn out perfectly everytime, but sometimes they don't, even if you're an experienced cook. Here are some of the most common problems and advice on how to avoid them next time.

PROBLEM: The cake sank in the centre.

POSSIBLE REASONS:
* The mixture was too runny.
* The oven door was opened too soon and for too long during the cooking process.
* The oven wasn't hot enough.
* The cake was not cooked for long enough.

PROBLEM: The cake burnt.

POSSIBLE REASONS:
* The cake was placed too near to the top of the oven. Always cook in the centre of the oven, even with fan ovens.
* The oven was too hot. No matter what it says on the temperature dial, ovens do vary. Next time, cook it on a slightly lower heat.

PROBLEM: The cake seemed very dry.

POSSIBLE REASONS:
* It was overcooked. Reduce the cooking time the next time you make it.
* There wasn't enough liquid in the mixture. If it's virtually impossible to stir the uncooked cake mixture, you need to add a dash more milk or egg.

PROBLEM: The fruit sank.

POSSIBLE REASONS:
* The oven door was opened for too long during cooking.
* There was too much flour in the mixture.

NUMBER AND LETTER CAKES

Thinking of new decorating ideas for birthday cakes year after year can be quite difficult. Creating number and letter shapes out of round or square cakes is very simple to do. The finished cake will always be appreciated by the recipients as it is very personal to them.

Numbers

The easiest way to bake a cake in the shape of a number is to buy or hire a cake tin in the shape of the required number (Fig. a). Most cake decorating and kitchen equipment shops offer this service. To work out how much cake mixture you will need, use the tip given on page 9 for calculating the amount required to fill an unusual shaped tin.

Grease the sides of the tin and line it with a strip of greaseproof paper. If the tin has a base, trace around the tin itself and cut out a piece to lay on the base of the tin. Stand the tin on a baking sheet when cooking so that the heat is evenly distributed along the base of the cake.

If you cannot obtain a number shaped tin, you can cut numbers out of square and round cakes instead (Fig. b). On pages 18–19 you will find a guide to show you how you can cut any number out of round and square cakes.

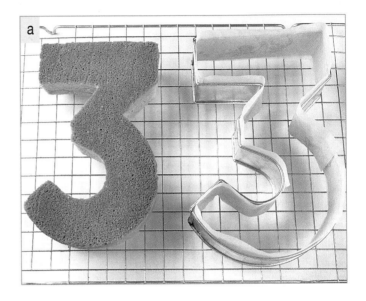

a

b

LEFT *A simple option is to decorate the cake with sweets arranged in a number on the top.*

RIGHT *One way to deal with "holes" in letters or numbers is to ignore them and to place a model or candles in the spot where a "hole" would normally be.*

Guide to cutting numbers out of square and round cakes.

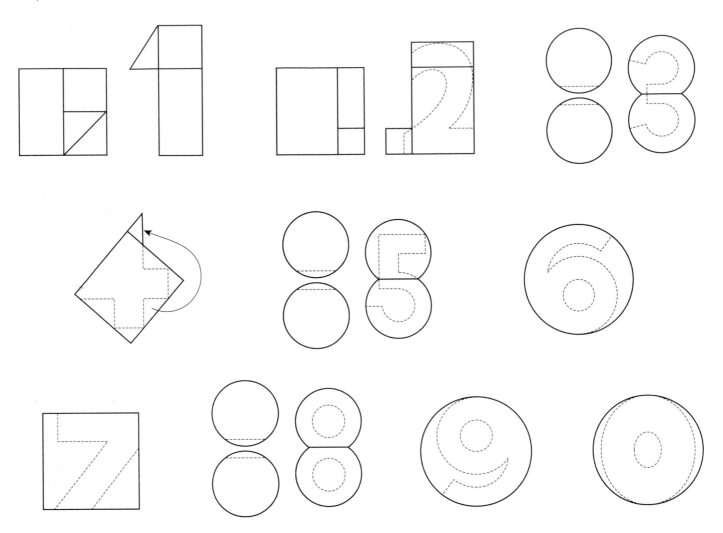

Decorating number-shaped cakes with buttercream

The easiest way to decorate an irregular shaped cake is to cover it with buttercream.

1 Slice the cake into layers as you would a round or square cake.

2 Re-assemble it, filling the layers with buttercream. Place on a cakeboard.

3 Spread buttercream around the sides and top (Fig. a) and decorate with sweets or other decorations of your choice.

a

Numbers with holes

To decorate a cake in the shape of a number with a hole in it, such as "6", you need to use a slightly different method.

1 Cut the cake into shape and slice into layers.

2 Cut a hole out of the top layer only.

3 Spread a little black buttercream in the centre of the next layer. Don't go right to the edge or the black buttercream will "leak" out of the sides when you reassemble the cake.

b

4 Spread your chosen colour of buttercream around the outside of the black buttercream on the lower layer and around the outside of the hole in the top layer (Fig. b).

5 Re-assemble the cake and spread buttercream around the sides and top of the cake. Pipe or stick sweets around the edges of the cake.

Decorating with sugarpaste

Simple rounded or straight numbers like "0" or "1" can normally be covered all in one go. Numbers with a lot of curved edges and corners, like "3" are more fiddly.

1 Slice and fill the cake with buttercream and place it in position on the cake board. Spread a thin coating of buttercream around the outside of the cake. This will ensure that the sugarpaste sticks to the cake.

2 Roll out the sugarpaste. Using the baking tin as a template, cut out an outline of the number and place it on top of the cake. Paint a light line of water around the cut edge of the sugarpaste topping.

3 Roll out some more sugarpaste and cut out a long thin strip. The width of the strip should be the same measurement as the height of the cake, including the sugarpaste topping.

4 Roll up the strip like a loose bandage and unroll it around the sides of the cake (Fig. c). To hide the joins, either pipe or crimp along the top edge of the cake (see page 65).

c

Letters

The same decorating techniques that were used for covering numbers can also be used to decorate letter-shaped cakes. You may be able to hire a letter-shaped cake tin from a cake decorating or kitchen shop. Alternatively, you can create your own out of round or square cakes. You can use any leftover bits of cake to make delicious truffles (see page 118).

RIGHT *"T" is a very simple shape to cut out of a square cake.*

Guide for cutting letters out of square and round cakes

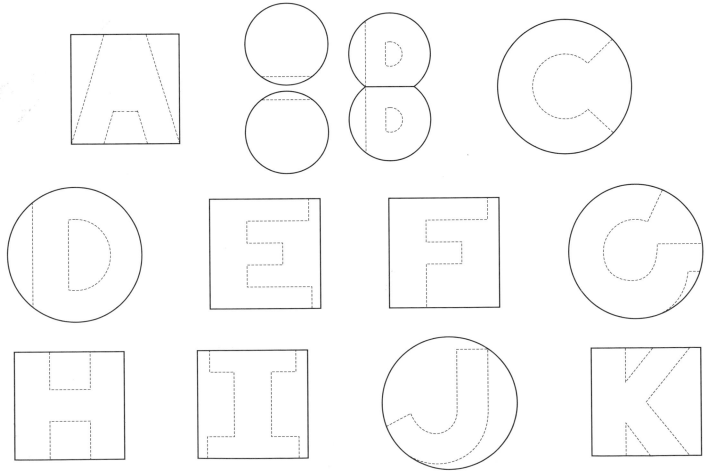

BASIC EQUIPMENT

It is not necessary to purchase everything listed here before you can decorate your first cake. A carving knife, rolling pin, small sharp knife, palette knife and paintbrush are the barest essentials. If you enjoy using sugarpaste, it would be worth buying a cake smoother, as using one dramatically improves the finish of the cake. Build up your collection gradually. A plastic workman's toolbox, which you can buy cheaply from a DIY store, is an ideal container for your tools.

TURNTABLE (1) Although not, strictly speaking, essential, once you've used one, you'll wonder what you ever did without it. Cheaper versions are available in plastic.

RULER (2) Not just for measuring; a ruler can also be useful for pressing lines and patterns into sugarpaste.

MEASURING SPOONS (3) A standard set ensures that you use the same quantities each time you make a recipe.

SCISSORS (4) A decent pair of sharp scissors is essential for making piping bags, cutting linings for tins and, sometimes, sugarpaste.

TAPE MEASURE (5) Useful for measuring cakes and boards to ensure that you have rolled out enough sugarpaste.

PIPING NOZZLES OR TIPS (6) A varied selection is always useful and they can double up as small circle cutters. Metal nozzles are more expensive than plastic but are sharper and more accurate.

SMALL DISHES (7) Useful for holding water when modelling; icing sugar when rolling out sugarpaste. Also ideal when mixing food colour into icing.

BAKING TINS (8) An assortment of shapes and sizes is useful.

SIEVE (STRAINER) (9) Vital for sifting flour and icing sugar. Also a useful tool for making bushes or hair by simply pushing a lump of sugarpaste through the mesh.

DRINKING STRAWS (10) These can be used as tiny circle cutters and are ideal for making eyes. Held at an angle and pressed into sugarpaste, they can also be used for making the scales on snakes, dinosaurs, etc.

COCKTAIL STICKS (11) For adding food colour to sugarpaste and for making frills and dotty patterns.

ROLLING PIN (12) A long rolling pin like the one shown will not leave handle dents in the sugarpaste. Tiny ones are also available and are useful for rolling out small quantities of sugarpaste when modelling. If you don't possess a small rolling pin, a paintbrush handle will often do the job just as well.

CAKE SMOOTHER (13) By using a smoother like an iron and running it over the surface of a covered cake, small bumps and lumps can literally be ironed out. Essential for achieving a smooth finish.

CUTTERS (14) A vast range of shapes is available in both plastic and metal.

COOLING RACK (15) Available in all shapes and sizes and used for cooling cakes.

MIXING AND PUDDING BOWLS (16 and 26) Essential for mixing cake mixture. Useful for mixing colours into icing and baking rounded cakes.

SMALL SHARP KNIFE (17) A small kitchen knife with a sharp, straight blade will become one of your most important pieces of equipment.

BOARD (18) Essential for protecting work surfaces.

PAINTBRUSHES (19) A medium brush is good for sticking things with water when modelling and cleaning out piping nozzles. A fine one is needed for adding delicate detail. Sable brushes are best.

SOFT PASTRY BRUSH (20) It is useful to have two brushes– one for dampening or cleaning large areas, the other for brushing away dusty fingerprints or specks of dried sugarpaste icing.

SCALPEL (21) Invaluable when careful cutting is required, such as when scribing around a template.

CARVING KNIFE (22) A long, sharp serrated knife is essential for shaping and slicing cakes.

PALETTE KNIFE (METAL SPATULA) (23) For spreading jam or buttercream, mixing colour into larger quantities of royal icing and lifting small bits of sugarpaste.

WOODEN SPOON (24) As well as stirring cake mixture, the handle can be used as a modelling tool.

GREASEPROOF PAPER (25) Used for lining tins, making piping bags and storing fruit cakes. Can be used in place of tracing paper.

Ribbons

A collection of ribbons is a must if you're going to take up cake decorating. They make fantastic instant decorations (see Christmas bows on page 102).

Often ribbon is placed around the edge of a cake board, particularly on cakes for special occasions. Double-sided tape is probably the best thing to use to secure the ribbon to the edge of the board as it does not bleed through the ribbon or taint the taste of the cake.

Instant decorations

Don't despair if you've left things to the last minute. Sweets, crystalized fruits, flowers, shop-bought sugar decorations and ribbon can all be used to make colourful instant decorations. Even a paper doily can be used to create an instant dramatic effect (see page 120).

Take a good look around your local cake decorating equipment shop or specialist kitchenware store. They will have many types of decoration in stock – some edible, some not. Your local supermarket is another good source; you should find a range of things including sprinkles, silver cake balls and chocolate leaves. Silk flowers are another great way of decorating a cake in double-quick time (see page 73).

Candles

Try to make candles part of the design. Use colours that tone with the cake. On novelty cakes, it might be possible to stand them in thick, cut-out shapes or balls of sugarpaste so that they tie in with the design. You can even stick the holders into marshmallows, then fix the marshmallows onto the board with dabs of royal icing or buttercream. Be very careful if you're using candles on cakes that use rice paper or silk flower decorations which are flammable. Position the candles well away from the decorations, light for the minimum amount of time and never leave unattended.

Pillars and stands

There are many different styles and designs of pillar. Some plain, some incredibly decorative. Although none of the cake designs in this book actually include pillars, here is a brief look at the basics of what they are and how to use them, in case you decide that you want to adapt one of the cake designs to include pillars.

The pillars have plastic dowels inside them (special plastic rods manufactured to comply with food regulations; available from cake decoration shops). Although the pillars might look sturdy it is the hidden dowels that bear the weight of the cakes above.

Cake stands

Cake stands are an easy way of displaying wedding cakes and are a great idea for the beginner as well as the professional. There are no pillars, dowels or measurements involved. All that is required is the ability to look up your nearest cake decoration shop or bakers in the telephone directory to see where you can hire one from.

There are many styles and designs available. They can range from two tiers to six or more. A two-tier stand was used for the Wedding star on page 104.

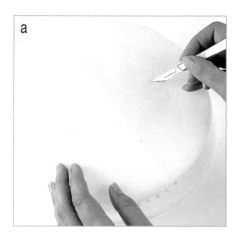

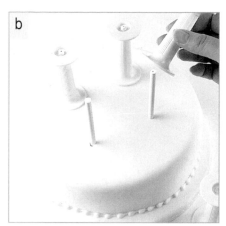

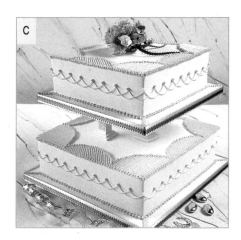

Using pillars on sugarpaste or buttercream cakes

1 Decide how many pillars you want – usually three or four. Make a template of the top of the cake by drawing around the tin it was baked in onto greaseproof paper.

2 Fold the template in half and half again. Unfold the paper and make a mark on one of the folds, the distance in from the edge of the cake you'd like the pillar to be. Make corresponding marks on the other folds.

3 Place the template on top of the cake and using something like a pin or tip of a scalpel, make a tiny mark through each of the dots onto the surface of the cake (Fig. a). Remove the template.

4 Measure the height of the cake and the height of the pillar and add the two measurements together. Make a mark on one of the cake dowels the same length as that joint measurement.

5 Using a serrated knife, make a little saw mark at that point on the dowel and then bend and snap the unwanted section off.

6 Slot the dowel into one of the marked positions on the cake. Slide the pillar on top. Repeat for all of the other pillars (Fig. b). Because they bear the weight of the cake above, it is essential that the top of the dowel is level with the top of the pillar. If it is lower, the pillar will be squashed down into the cake beneath.

Using pillars on royal-iced cakes

There are various ways of using pillars on a traditional royal-iced fruit cake, but below I have detailed the simplest, quickest method. To prepare the cakes, cover each fruit cake with marzipan and a minimum of three thin coatings of royal icing. Allow each coating to dry thoroughly before applying the next. It is essential that the top of each iced cake is flat and level. Use a small spirit level to check. Fig. c shows a two-tier cake.

When the iced cake has dried, make marks on the cake's surface for the pillars. Scratch a hole into the icing at each of these points using the tip of a scalpel or scriber. The hole needs to be big enough to accommodate a cake dowel. Then follow steps 4 to 6 for Using pillars on sugarpaste or buttercream cakes.

How easy?

All of the cakes in this book can be made successfully by a beginner, but, obviously, there are some cakes that are simpler than others. You will notice that each cake has been allocated a number. This is a quick reference guide to give you a rough idea of how involved the design is and therefore how much time it is likely to take you.

1 Easy

2 Fairly easy

3 Has intricate elements

BUTTERCREAM ICING

Buttercream is probably the easiest type of icing to both make and use. Made from a mixture of butter, icing sugar and a little water, it can be used to fill and cover cakes, and for piping and making decorations.

Recipe

Making up a batch of buttercream will only take you a few minutes.

ingredients

(Amounts for 1 quantity)

250g (8oz) softened butter, preferably unsalted

500g (1lb) icing sugar

1 tbsp boiled, hot water

1 tsp vanilla essence

1 Beat the butter until soft and fluffy.

2 Add the sugar, water and essence. Beat until pale and creamy.

Different flavours

White or milk chocolate
Stir either 100g (3½oz) melted white or plain chocolate, or 1 tablespoon cocoa powder mixed to a paste with about 1–2 tablespoons of hot water, into the buttercream.

Coffee
Mix about 1 tablespoon of instant coffee into 1 tablespoon of water and beat into the buttercream.

Flavoured essences
You can use vanilla, peppermint, lemon or almond essence to flavour buttercream. Just add a few drops and mix in.

Colouring buttercream

It is best to use paste colours as they are not as runny as liquid ones. Liquid colours can be used with buttercream but because of their consistency you will only be able to tint the icing lightly. If it starts to get too soggy and out of control, add more icing sugar.

As buttercream has a naturally creamy colour, some colours like pale blue and pale pink will never be quite as true as they would be were the colours being mixed into pure white royal icing. However, if you beat and beat and beat buttercream (and you'll need a food mixer for this otherwise your arm will drop off!) it will eventually turn almost white and will take very pale colours a little better. The other thing to remember when you are adding colour is that the shade will deepen as the buttercream sets.

1 Add the colour using a cocktail stick (Fig. a).

2 Mix into the buttercream, ensuring that it is blended evenly (Fig. b).

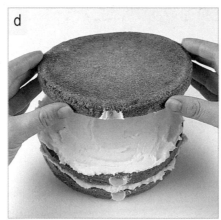

Freezing buttercream

Buttercream freezes extremely well. This quality is exploited in the frozen buttercream transfer cakes on pages 50–51 and 54–55.

If you are covering a cake and find that you have a lot of buttercream left over, it can be placed in a bag or plastic container and frozen until the next baking day comes round. Let it defrost at room temperature for a few hours, then give it a stir. As with all foods, never refreeze buttercream once it has been defrosted.

Another useful fact is that because both sponge cake and buttercream freeze well, you can actually freeze a ready-buttercreamed cake. Protect it with freezer wrap. Defrosting will take anything from 5–12 hours depending upon the room temperature. Condensation will form as it defrosts but avoid the temptation to dab it, the cake will dry naturally. Occasionally, strong colours such as black may run a little.

Filling the cake

Have you ever sliced a cake up, filled it with buttercream, put it back together again and found that none of the layers now seem to fit properly? Here's a little trick to stop that happening.

1 Before you slice the cake into layers, make a buttercream mark down the side of the cake (Fig. c). You can mark it with a knife cut, but I prefer to use buttercream as I tend to lose the cut mark in a flurry of crumbs!

2 Slice your cake into layers and spread buttercream over the top of the base layer. Place the next layer on top of the bottom one – and here's the trick – line the buttercream marks up with each other. If you have a third layer, repeat the procedure, again lining the buttercream marks up (Fig. d).

3 Ensure that the layers are even (Fig. e).

Covering with buttercream

When covering a cake with buttercream, cover the sides first. This allows you to hold the top of the cake steady with your other hand without getting too sticky. Spread the buttercream around the sides and over the top (Fig. f).

"Setting up" and avoiding crumbs

If you coat your cake with a thin covering of buttercream then place it in the refrigerator for a couple of hours to "set up" before covering it with a second, final coating, you will help yourself in two ways. Firstly, it prevents crumbs from being dragged around the surface of the cake. Secondly, it stops the cake from moving as you buttercream it. This is especially useful when coating tall cakes such as the Puppet on a string and Candy house (see pages 44–45 and 46–47).

Special effects

There are many different effects you can achieve in butter-cream through using different techniques, tools and colours.

Combing

An icing comb is a plastic tool with a serrated edge. As it is run around the outside of a cake, a combed effect is left behind (see Summer flowers on pages 48–49). If it is wiggled as it is moved around the cake, it will produce a zigzag pattern (see Who's looking at you? on pages 58–59).

If you want to experiment with combing but don't have a comb, you can very easily make your own. Cut a rectangle out of an ice cream container lid. Cut a few triangles out of one side and you have a homemade icing comb.

Marbling

By partially mixing a little food colour into the buttercream you get a marbled effect – great for making water effects on novelty cakes.

Multi-coloured swirls and piping

Achieve a dramatic effect by swirling different colours of buttercream on to a cake's surface (see picture below left).

You can also pipe with two or three different colours in the piping bag at the same time (Figs a and b).

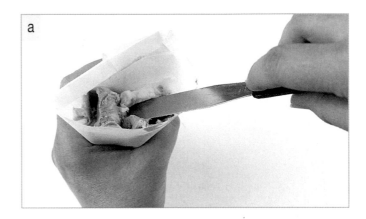

a

b

Piping

It is very easy to pipe with buttercream provided that the icing is soft enough to flow easily through the piping nozzle but still holds its shape when piped. If it is too stiff, beat in a little more water.

Because piping with buttercream and royal icing is similar, piping and lettering techniques are described fully in the royal icing section on pages 96–100.

Templates

All of the templates on pages 29–31 are shown at 100%.

Baby face (pages 50–51)

Spring blossom (pages 54–55)

Pretty butterflies (pages 38–39)

Buttercream beauty (pages 56–57)

Figure

Border

Celebration cake ①

The ice cream wafer sticks used here add a pretty pattern to the cake as well as being extremely easy to do. You could substitute chocolate finger biscuits if you prefer.

ingredients

20-cm (8-in) round sponge cake (see page 10)

2 quantities vanilla buttercream (see page 26)

Small, round, sugar-coated chocolate sweets

Green food colour paste

About 54 ice cream wafer fingers (approximately 3 packs)

equipment

Carving knife

Palette knife

Cake board

Piping bag (see page 96, but read the tip opposite first)

Scissors

No. 3 piping nozzle

1m (36in) lilac ribbon

techniques

Covering a cake with buttercream page 27

Colouring buttercream page 26

Making a piping bag page 97

Piping page 98

1 Split the cake horizontally two or three times and re-assemble it, sandwiching the layers together with buttercream.

2 Place the cake onto the cake board and spread a thick covering of buttercream around the outside of the cake.

3 Place yellow sweets – which will form the centres of the flowers – in position on the cake. Make sure there is enough space between them to fit in all the petals.

4 Place six pink or purple sweets around each yellow centre to form the flowers (Fig. a).

5 To make the leaves, place about a tablespoon of green buttercream in a piping bag. Snip a triangle off the end of the bag. Insert a number 3 piping nozzle and then place 1 tablespoon of green buttercream into the bag. Fold the bag to close.

6 Pipe a leaf between each flower. Simply squeeze some icing out of the end of the bag between two petals. Then release the pressure on the bag and pull away. The icing should fall away forming a tail (Fig. b).

7 Fill the spaces between the flowers with a few additional sweets.

8 Press the ice cream wafers around the outside of the cake and finish with a ribbon trim. Use a dab of buttercream to secure the ribbon at the back of the cake.

tip

If you don't have time to do piping or you really don't like doing it, use small bits of angelica or green jelly sweets instead to make the leaves.

buttercream icing

Silver wedding cake ❶

Sometimes you're in a hurry or perhaps you've been asked to make an important cake but you've never even wielded a rolling pin before let alone a piping bag. Well you're in luck! Most kitchen and cake decorating shops stock all sorts of ready-made decorations. These silver paper rose leaves link beautifully with a silver wedding theme and look lovely and sparkly too. Even better, there's not a piping bag in sight!

ingredients
18-cm (7-in) square sponge cake (see page 10)
1 quantity vanilla buttercream (see page 26)
Edible silver balls

equipment
Carving knife
Palette knife
23-cm (9-in) square cake board
13–15cm (5–6in) diameter bowl
Tweezers (optional; see tip opposite)
About 64 silver paper rose leaves
1m (36in) silver ribbon
Scissors

techniques
Covering a cake with buttercream page 27

1 Turn the cake upside down. If it won't sit flat on your work surface, turn it back over and slice the top to make it level, then turn it over again.

2 Slice the cake horizontally into two or three layers. Reassemble it, sandwiching the layers together with buttercream.

3 Place the cake on the board and spread buttercream around the outside of the cake.

4 Carefully place a bowl upside down on the top of the iced cake and just as carefully, lift it off. It should have left a circular impression in the icing (Fig. a).

5 Using the impression as a guide, stick a circle of silver balls around the top of the cake (Fig. b).

6 Stick the silver rose leaves around the top edge and base of the cake. Make a ribbon bow and place it in the centre. Finally, press a few additional balls into the icing around the cake.

tip
You may find it easier to use a pair of tweezers to handle the silver balls – they can be a bit fiddly.

a

b

Teddy bear 1

This cute teddy is very easy to do. If you don't want to use marzipan for the eyes and ears you could use sweets and chocolate buttons for the eyes and nose and small round biscuits for the cheeks and ears.

ingredients

20-cm (8-in) square sponge cake (see page 10)
1 quantity chocolate buttercream (see page 26)
100g (3½oz) golden marzipan
1 tbsp cocoa powder (or brown food colour paste)

equipment

Carving knife
Palette knife
30-cm (12-in) round cake board
Fork
1m (36in) red ribbon
Scissors

techniques

Covering a cake with buttercream page 27
Creating effects with buttercream page 28
Colouring marzipan page 88

1 Slice about 5cm (2in) off one side of the square cake to make it rectangular. Place the piece you have cut off against the top of the cake to form a "T" shape.

2 Cut out the teddy shape (see tips below). The head should be rounded, coming into a point at the neck (Fig. a).

3 Slice the cake and fill with buttercream. Place onto the cake board. Spread a thick buttercream coating around the outside of the cake. Use a fork to rough it up to look like fur (Fig. b).

4 Colour about 45g (1½oz) marzipan brown by kneading in the cocoa powder or food colour.

5 Make three 5g (⅛oz) dark brown balls for the eyes and nose. Add tiny balls of uncoloured marzipan for the highlights. If the highlights won't stick, use a dab of water to hold them in place.

6 Roll out and squash two 15g (½oz) balls of uncoloured marzipan to make two flattened circles for the cheeks. Place them in position.

7 Add the eyes and the nose. Decorate both cheeks with three tiny flattened brown marzipan dots and add a curved marzipan string for a mouth.

8 To make the ears, roll 30g (1oz) brown marzipan and 15g (½oz) uncoloured marzipan into balls. Place the smaller one on top of the larger one and flatten them both together. Cut the flat disc in half and stick one ear either side of the head.

9 Finish the teddy bear off with a snazzy red bow.

tips

If you are unsure about cutting directly into the cake to make the teddy bear shape, make a template first out of greaseproof paper. Place this on top of the cake and cut around it.

Stand birthday cake candles in their holders in balls of marzipan or regular-sized marshmallows (see page 24). With a dab of water, stick these around the cake board away from the cake (particularly the ribbon bow).

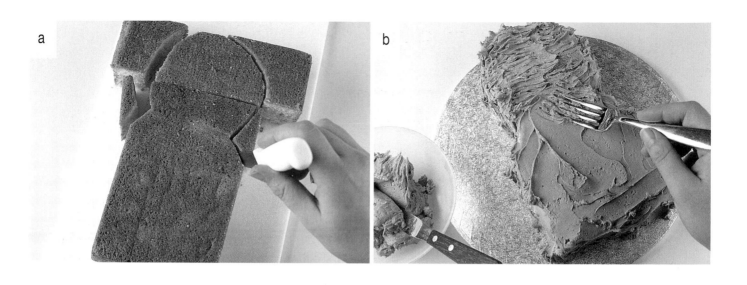

Pretty butterflies ❶

An elegant yet simple design that would be suitable for Valentine's Day, an anniversary or a birthday. If you don't want to make it heart-shaped, the butterflies work just as well on square and round cakes.

ingredients

5–6 sheets rice paper

Edible dusting powders in assorted
    colours

2 tbsp icing sugar

18-cm (7-in) square sponge cake (see
    page 10)

2 quantities pink buttercream (see
    page 26)

equipment

Scissors

Pencil

Saucer

Greaseproof or tracing paper

Carving knife

Palette knife

25-cm (10-in) round cake board

techniques

Colouring buttercream page 26

Covering a cake with buttercream page 27

1 To make the butterflies you can just cut them out freehand or use the templates supplied on page 30. If cutting freehand, simply fold a piece of rice paper in half and cut out half a butterfly shape. If using the templates, make sure that the edge of the template lines up with the rice paper fold. Cut inside the pencil lines (Fig. a). Open out the butterfly and place to one side. Make about 40.

2 To colour the butterflies, place some dusting powders on the edge of a saucer and some icing sugar in the centre. Using your finger, mix a little dusting powder with a little icing sugar and spread onto a butterfly's wings using a light circular motion (see Fig. a, page 57). If the rice paper is rough side up, a textured effect will appear. Colour the rice paper on one side only. Decorate all of the butterflies and place to one side.

3 Trace around the heart-shaped cake template on page 67 and cut out. Place the template on top of the cake and cut out the shape (Fig. b).

4 Slice the cake into two or three layers and sandwich the layers together with buttercream. Place the cake on the board and spread a thick covering of buttercream around the top and sides.

5 Gently press the butterflies into the buttercream all over the cake.

tips

You can prepare your butterflies weeks ahead if you wish.

Be very careful if using candles on a cake like this as the rice paper could easily catch fire. If you really want to use candles stick butterflies around the sides of the cake only and place the candles on top.

a

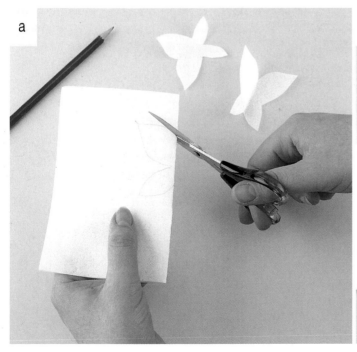

b

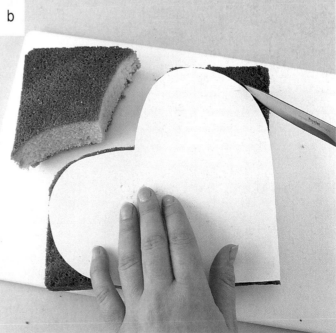

Take the train ❶

Incredible though it may seem, there is absolutely no baking involved in this cake – it can all be bought from the supermarket (although you can use your own baked cakes if you wish). The only thing you need to make is some buttercream for sticking the elements together.

ingredients

6 mini chocolate Swiss rolls
1 quantity buttercream (see page 26)
1 large chocolate Swiss roll
1 Battenburg cake (or similar – any rectangular chunk of cake will do!)
7 plain, round biscuits
2 white chocolate buttons
Assorted small, round, coloured sweets
1 red jelly bean
About 14 chocolate finger biscuits
1 mini jam Swiss roll
2 breadsticks
30g (1oz) desiccated coconut
Black and green food colour pastes

equipment

25-cm (10-in) square cake board
Carving knife
Palette knife
Fork

techniques

Colouring buttercream page 26
Creating effects with buttercream page 28

1 Place six mini Swiss rolls in a diagonal line on the cake board. Fix in place with dabs of buttercream.

2 Place the large Swiss roll on top so that it overhangs the rolls at the front. Leave enough room at the other end to stand the Battenburg cake up, so trim the Swiss roll to size if necessary. The roll represents the engine.

3 Stand the Battenburg cake upright on the mini rolls, behind the engine and fix in place with buttercream (Fig. a). The Battenburg cake is the driver's cab.

4 Stick three plain biscuits along both sides of the engine to form the wheels. Stick another one on the front of the train ready for the face.

5 To make the face, use two white chocolate buttons and two small round brown sweets for the eyes. Use a pink sweet for the nose and a red jellybean for the mouth. Stick in place with buttercream (Fig. b).

6 Stick about six chocolate fingers on top of the driver's cab and sweets around the edges of the engine and cab.

7 Stick a mini jam roll funnel upright on top of the engine and a breadstick horizontally along each set of wheels.

8 Use about four chocolate fingers to make short sections of track in front of and behind the train. Fix in place with buttercream (Fig. c).

9 Place the coconut into a bowl and mix some black food colour into it using a spoon or your fingers. Carefully sprinkle the coloured coconut "gravel" between the tracks. (You can leave this step out if you find it too fiddly.)

10 Colour the leftover buttercream green and smear it around the rest of the board. Use a fork to rough it up a little to resemble grass.

tips

If you're feeling really ambitious you could paint a food colour face on a sweet or directly on to the marzipan on the front of the cab to look like the driver.

Stand birthday cake candles in holders in regular-sized marshmallows and press these into the grass, well away from the train.

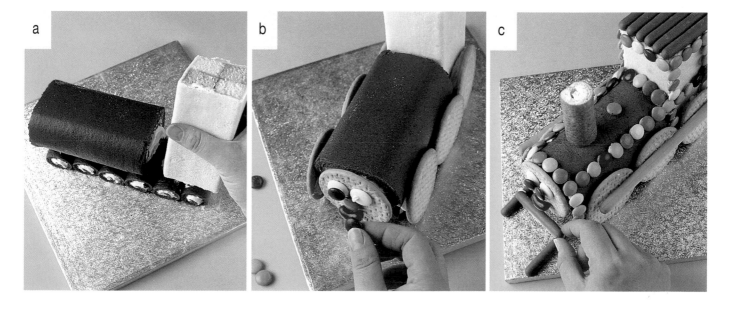

a

b

c

Buttercream flowers ❷

This star piping technique is easy to master and produces an interesting texture as well as an attractive design. This cake would be suitable for all sorts of occasions – birthdays, Mother's day, Easter – to name but a few.

ingredients

18-cm (7-in) round sponge cake (see page 10)

2 quantities vanilla buttercream (see page 26)

1 strand raw, dried spaghetti or similar

Pink, yellow, green food colour pastes

equipment

Carving knife

Palette knife

23-cm (9-in) round cake board

Star piping nozzles

Piping bags (see page 96)

Small bowls for mixing colours

techniques

Layering and filling a cake page 27

Colouring buttercream page 26

Making a piping bag page 97

Piping stars page 98

1 Level the top of the cake and turn it upside-down. Split the cake horizontally and fill the layers with buttercream.

2 Place the cake onto the cake board and spread a thin coating of buttercream over the outside of the cake.

3 Using a strand of spaghetti, gently score the outline of the pattern you are going to pipe into the buttercream. If you go wrong, smooth the buttercream over and start again. Draw wiggly lines for the stems and a circle surrounded by petals for the flowers (Fig. a). These lines will be hidden by the piping .

4 Place a star nozzle into a piping bag. Put about a tablespoon of pink icing into the bag and fold the end of the bag to close it.

5 Pipe a star on the edge of one of the flower centres. Just squeeze a bit of icing out of the end of the nozzle, release the pressure and pull the bag upwards, away from the cake. Pipe a ring of stars around the outside of one of the flower centres then fill in the middle. Repeat on the other two flower centres (Fig. b).

6 Repeat the procedure on the flower petals using yellow buttercream. Then pipe and fill in the stems and the leaves with green. Finally, fill in the outside of the cake using uncoloured buttercream.

7 To decorate the board, pipe a line of green stars around the base of the cake. Follow this with a ring of uncoloured buttercream, then a line of pink.

8 To finish, pipe a few single pink stars over the cake.

tip

This cake can be decorated and then frozen. Store it carefully in the freezer to avoid damage and defrost gently at room temperature for 6–8 hours.

a
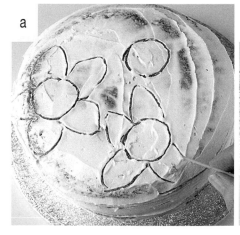

b
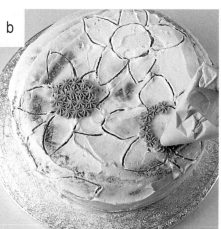

Puppet on a string ❷

Now admit it, you never knew a breadstick could be this useful did you? Here they make great handles for dangling a puppet on a string.

ingredients

20-cm (8-in) square sponge cake (see
    page 10)
1 quantity vanilla buttercream (see
    page 26)
2 breadsticks
4 lollipops
Liquorice bootlace sweets
1 ice cream cone
1 round biscuit
2 strands of thicker lace sweets for hair
White and milk chocolate buttons
Assorted sweets for decorating cake
    and board

equipment

Carving knife
20-cm (8-in) square cake board
Palette knife
Scissors
Small sharp knife

techniques

Covering a cake with buttercream page 27
"Setting up" page 28

tips

To make a boy puppet use a second round biscuit to make a body instead of the dress. Decorate with a couple of chocolate buttons. Give him shorter hair and leave the bow off.

Either stand birthday cake candles in holders on the top of the cake or stand the holders in marshmallows and stick them onto the cake board with buttercream.

1 Slice about 5cm (2in) off one side of the square cake to form a 20 × 15cm (8 × 6in) rectangle.

2 Stand the cake upright on one of the shorter sides. Use what was originally the flat base of the cake to form a smooth front.

3 If you want to fill the cake with buttercream, slice the cake horizontally into two or three layers and reassemble it with buttercream filling.

4 Stand the cake diagonally on the cake board and spread buttercream over the sides and top.

5 If you have time, place the cake in the fridge for about an hour so that the buttercream can harden. Spread another coating of buttercream over the outside of the cake when you remove it from the fridge so that the sweets have something to stick to.

6 Lay two crossed breadsticks on top of the cake. Use dabs of buttercream to hold them in place.

7 Press two lollipops into the lower part of the cake for the legs.

8 Cut two pieces of liquorice bootlace, about 25cm (10in) long, for the strings. Press them into the cake so that they run from a lollipop foot, up the cake and over the top of the breadsticks. Trim if necessary and press the ends into the buttercream on top of the cake (Fig. a).

9 Carefully cut the pointed end off an ice cream cone and slice the cone in half. Place it over the top of the legs to form a dress. Add a biscuit for the head (Fig. b).

10 Add two more lollipops for arms and bootlace strings leading from the arms and head to the breadsticks.

11 Use a couple of thicker, sugar lace sweets to make the hair, pressing them gently into the buttercream so that they stay in place.

12 Use two white and two milk chocolate buttons for the eyes. Stick them onto the biscuit face with dabs of buttercream. Add a tiny buttercream dot for a highlight (Fig. c).

13 For the mouth cut a milk chocolate button in half and stick in place. Cut four white chocolate buttons in half. Use two to make the collar and five to make a frill around the bottom of the dress. Stick two milk chocolate buttons on the front of the dress. Make a bootlace bow and stick it on top of the head.

14 Smear the cake board with buttercream and press sweets all around the outside edges of the cake and over the cake board.

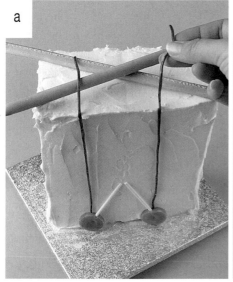
a

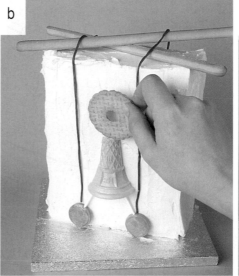
b

c

Candy house ❷

Just watch your child's face light up with delight when this fairytale house arrives on the table. It may look terribly complicated at first glance but in fact it is very easy to assemble. If you are planning to incorporate candles into the design, please read the tip below before you start.

ingredients

25-cm (10-in) square sponge cake (see page 10)

1 quantity buttercream (see page 26; colour 4 tbsp green for the grass, flavour the rest with chocolate)

Green food colour paste

Milk and white chocolate finger biscuits

3 thin slices Battenburg cake or square biscuits

At least 15 ice cream wafers

Assorted small sweets and mini marshmallows for brickwork

1 mini Swiss roll

Raindrop sweets or sugar strands for gravel

Coconut mushrooms

equipment

Carving knife

Palette knife

30-cm (12in) round cake board

Fork

tip

To incorporate candles safely, make sure that the house is positioned at the back of the cakeboard and only use the chocolate finger fencing around the back and sides of the house. Stick the candles into holders and insert the holders into regular-sized marshmallows. Stand the candles around the edge of the board as far away from the house as possible.

1 If your cake has a very rounded top, slice a bit off to level it, then cut the entire cake in half diagonally.

2 Place the two triangular halves on top of each other. Slice a small triangle off each end (Fig. a).

3 Sandwich the layers together with buttercream. Stand the cake upright on the board and spread a thin coating of buttercream over the outside of the cake (Fig. b). If you have time, place the cake in the refrigerator for an hour.

4 Spread a second, thicker layer of buttercream over the outside of the cake. This will act as glue for the decorations.

5 Place four milk chocolate fingers upright in the centre to make a door. Press three thin slices of Battenburg cake or square biscuits in position for the windows. Add a couple of white chocolate fingers for steps and window ledges.

6 Then starting from the bottom, stick a line of overlapping wafers up both sides of the roof (Fig. c). Press one ice cream wafer over the door to make a porch.

7 Fill in the brickwork by pressing sweets or mini marshmallows into the buttercream around the house. If you want to save a bit of time and use less sweets, leave the back of the house plain, covered with buttercream only.

8 To make the chimney, slice a small diagonal section off a mini Swiss roll. Stick it on the roof with a blob of buttercream and add a small sweet for the chimney pot.

9 Stick a line of sweets along the ridge of the roof and a sweet for a doorknob. Decorate the roof with a few additional sweets if you wish. Again, use buttercream as glue.

10 Smear the green buttercream around the cake board. Use a fork to rough up the icing to make it look like grass.

11 To make the fencing, cut about 15 white chocolate fingers in half and stand them upright in the grass all around the house.

12 Sprinkle raindrop sweets or sugar strands in front of the door to make a path.

13 Place a few extra sweets or coconut mushrooms in the garden.

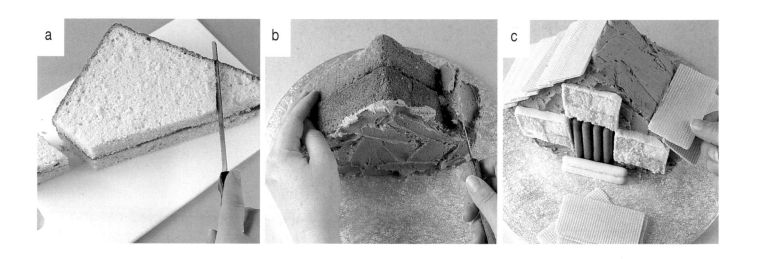

Summer flowers ❷

All the piping on this cake was done using a number 4 piping nozzle which has got a large round hole in the end. If you don't have one, you can achieve a similar effect by making a piping bag, filling it and snipping a tiny triangle off the end.

ingredients

2 quantities buttercream (see page 26)
15-cm (6-in) round sponge cake
   (see page 10)
Yellow, pink, green food colour pastes

equipment

Piping bags (see page 96)
No. 4 piping nozzle
Greaseproof or waxed paper
Carving knife
Palette knife
20-cm (8-in) round cake board
Small bowls for mixing colours
Serrated icing comb (optional)

techniques

Making a piping bag page 97
Filling and covering a cake with buttercream
   page 27
Colouring buttercream page 26
"Setting up" page 28
Combing a cake page 28

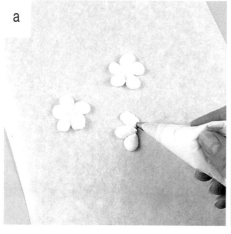

a

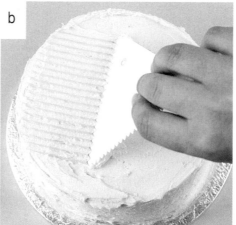

b

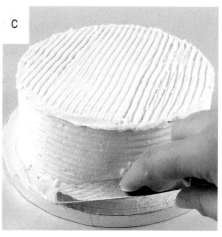

c

1 Place about 2 tablespoons of buttercream in a piping bag fitted with the number 4 piping nozzle. Pipe five large dots on to greaseproof paper in a flower formation (Fig. a). Make about 30 and leave to set in the fridge for a few hours.

2 In the meantime, prepare the cake. Split the cake into two or three layers and re-assemble it, filling the layers with buttercream. Colour all but 5 tablespoons of the rest of the buttercream yellow.

3 Place the cake on the board and spread a thin coating of yellow buttercream all over the outside of the cake. Put in the fridge for an hour or so to "set up". This will stop crumbs from getting caught up in the icing and spoiling the finish of the cake later.

4 When ready, spread a thicker coating of yellow buttercream over the sides. Run a serrated icing comb around the sides of the cake (optional).

5 Spread additional yellow buttercream over the top of the cake and run the icing comb over it (optional; Fig. b).

6 Using a palette knife, spread a thin coating of yellow buttercream over the cake board (Fig. c).

7 When the flowers are set, carefully lift them off the greaseproof paper with a knife and stick around the top edge of the cake with a blob of buttercream. Stick a cluster of three in the centre and the rest around the base of the cake.

8 Colour about a tablespoon of buttercream pink and place in a piping bag with the number 4 piping nozzle. Fold the bag to close. Pipe five dots in the centre of each flower. Wash the nozzle.

9 Colour the rest of the buttercream green and place in another piping bag with the number 4 piping nozzle. To pipe the leaves between the flowers, simply squeeze the bag, release the pressure and pull away. The icing will fall away, leaving a tapering tail behind.

variation

This version still conveys a feeling of freshness even though it has a lot less flowers on it. There is no combing involved and just three flowers in the centre. Leaves were piped around the top and base of the cake. Pink dots, in groups of three, were then piped both amongst the leaves and around the top and sides of the cake.

Baby face ❷

This technique called "frozen buttercream transfer" is a simple way to put pictures on top of cakes. Note that you will need to have a freezer in order to make the transfer. This would make a cute Christening cake or a first birthday cake.

ingredients

2 quantities buttercream (see page 26)

Black, pink, yellow, blue food colour pastes

15-cm (6-in) square sponge cake (see page 10)

4 packets small jelly sweets

equipment

Pencil

Greaseproof or tracing paper

Scissors

2 thin cake boards or pieces of card (bigger than the design)

Cling film, greaseproof or waxed paper

Adhesive tape

Piping bags (see page 96)

No. 2 piping nozzle

Small bowls for mixing colours

Dressmaker's pin

Carving knife

Palette knife

techniques

Making a piping bag page 97

Colouring buttercream page 26

Piping page 98

Filling and covering a cake with buttercream page 27

1 Trace the baby design on page 29 onto greaseproof or tracing paper. If you want to make a cake of a different size, use a photocopier to alter the size of the design.

2 Place the design onto a thin cake board and put a sheet of cling film over the top. Use a tiny bit of tape at the edges to hold it in place if you wish.

3 Place about a tablespoon of black buttercream into a piping bag fitted with a number 2 piping nozzle. Trace the picture and fill in the baby's mouth (see Fig. a page 55).

4 Place some pink buttercream in a piping bag. Close the end and snip a tiny triangle off the pointed end. Fill in the outline of the picture (see Fig. b page 55). Refer to the photograph opposite to help you put the colours in the right places.

5 Repeat the procedure with the blue and yellow buttercream and fill in the background of the picture with uncoloured buttercream.

6 When you have finished the picture, carefully remove the tape from the corners and gently lay a second sheet of cling film over the top of the design.

7 Place a second thin cake board on top of the pile and carefully turn the whole lot over. Gently press down and squash the boards together.

8 Remove what is now the top board and the traced design. Using your finger, gently rub over the cling film in a circular motion to get rid of the piping marks (Fig. a). Prick any air bubbles with a pin.

9 When you have finished, place the second cake board back on top of the picture and place in the freezer for at least an hour.

10 Cut the cake in half horizontally and sandwich the layers together with buttercream. Place the cake onto the cake board and spread a smooth covering of buttercream over the top and sides of the cake.

11 When frozen, remove the board and cling film from the back of the design.

12 Carefully lift the design by the edges of the cling film and lay the buttercreamed side on top of the cake. Peel off the cling film (Fig. b).

13 Spread buttercream over the cakeboard and press a line of jelly sweets around the edges of the cake. Place a few sweets in the corners and at the sides of the cake, and scatter some on the board.

a

b

Bouquet of hyacinths ❷

This cake is a perfect demonstration of how limiting the number of colours on a cake can actually enhance the design. If in doubt, keep it simple. Practise piping the stars a few times first before you attempt the real thing.

ingredients

15-cm (6-in) round sponge cake (see page 10)

2 quantities buttercream (see page 26)

Green, purple, blue food colour pastes

equipment

Carving knife

Palette knife

20-cm (8-in) round cake board

No. 4 piping nozzle

Scissors

Piping bags (see page 96)

Small bowls for mixing colours

Star piping nozzle

techniques

Filling and covering a cake with buttercream page 27

Colouring buttercream page 26

Making a piping bag page 97

Piping stars page 98

1 Level the top of the cake and split it horizontally into two or three layers. Re-assemble the cake, filling the layers with buttercream.

2 Place the cake on the cake board and spread buttercream around the top and sides.

3 Place the number 4 piping nozzle in a piping bag. Colour about 2 tablespoons of buttercream green and place in the bag. Fold over the end of the bag to close it and pipe lines for the stems and leaves around the sides of the cake (Fig. a). Pipe a cluster of stems and leaves on top of the cake.

4 Colour about 2 tablespoons of buttercream purple and place in a bag fitted with the star piping nozzle. Pipe a line of stars either side of one of the stems on top of the cake (Fig. b). Repeat on alternate flower stems all around the sides of the cake.

5 When you have piped all of the purple flowers, pipe a line of stars around the top edge of the cake.

variation

You can use the same star piping technique to make simple daisy flowers too. Pipe a central yellow star, then pipe five or six pink ones around the outside.

6 Wash and dry the star piping nozzle and place into a second piping bag. Colour about 2 tablespoons of buttercream blue and place into the bag. Pipe the remaining flowers and ring on top of cake (Fig. c).

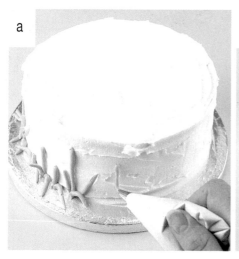

a

b

c

Spring blossom ❷

This cake is made using the same frozen transfer method as Baby face (see page 50), but piping and combing techniques are also used (see tip below).

ingredients

2 quantities buttercream (see page 26)

Black, yellow, pink, green, brown food colour pastes

18-cm (7-in) round sponge cake (see page 10)

equipment

Pencil

Greaseproof or tracing paper

Scissors

2 thin cake boards or pieces of card (bigger than the design)

Cling film, greaseproof or waxed paper

Adhesive tape

Piping bags (see page 96)

No. 2 and star piping nozzles

Small bowls for mixing colours

Dressmaker's pin

Carving knife

Palette knife

Serrated icing comb (optional)

techniques

Colouring buttercream page 26

Making a piping bag page 97

Piping page 98

Filling and covering a cake with buttercream page 27

Combing page 28

1 Trace the flower design on page 30 on to greaseproof or tracing paper. If you want to make a cake of a different size, alter the size of the design using a photocopier.

2 Place the design onto a thin cake board and place a sheet of cling film over the top. Use a tiny bit of tape at the edges to hold it in place.

3 Place about a tablespoon of black buttercream into a piping bag fitted with a number 2 piping nozzle. Pipe over the outline of the picture (Fig. a).

4 Place some yellow buttercream in a piping bag. Close and snip a tiny triangle off the end. Fill in the design using the appropriate colours (Fig. b). Use uncoloured buttercream for the background.

5 Carefully remove the tape from the corners and gently lay a second sheet of cling film over the top of the design. Place a second thin cake board on top of the pile and carefully turn the whole lot over. Gently press down and squash the boards together.

6 Remove what are now the top board and the traced design. Using your finger, gently rub the cling film in a circular motion to get rid of the piping marks (see Fig. a page 51). Use a pin to prick any air bubbles that might develop.

7 Place the second cake board back on top and put in the freezer for at least an hour.

8 Cut the cake in half horizontally and sandwich the layers together with buttercream. Place the cake on to the cake board and spread quite a thick coating of buttercream over the sides of the cake. If you wish, run an icing comb around the outside of the cake to make a pattern (see Fig. b page 49). Spread a thin buttercream coating over the top of the cake.

9 When the design has frozen, take it out of the freezer and remove the top board and sheet of cling film from the back of the design.

10 Carefully lift the design by the edges of the film and lay the buttercreamed side on top of the cake. Peel off the film (see Fig. b page 51).

11 Pipe a line of shells around the top and bottom edges of the cake and pipe a few pink stars on the side if you wish. You could use sweets instead if you prefer.

tip

To simplify this design, stick sweets around the edges of the cake instead of piping and combing.

Buttercream beauty ③

This cake may look intricate, but it's actually very easy to put together.
The design is simply cut out of rice paper and slotted into the buttercream
covering. The decorations can be made weeks in advance.

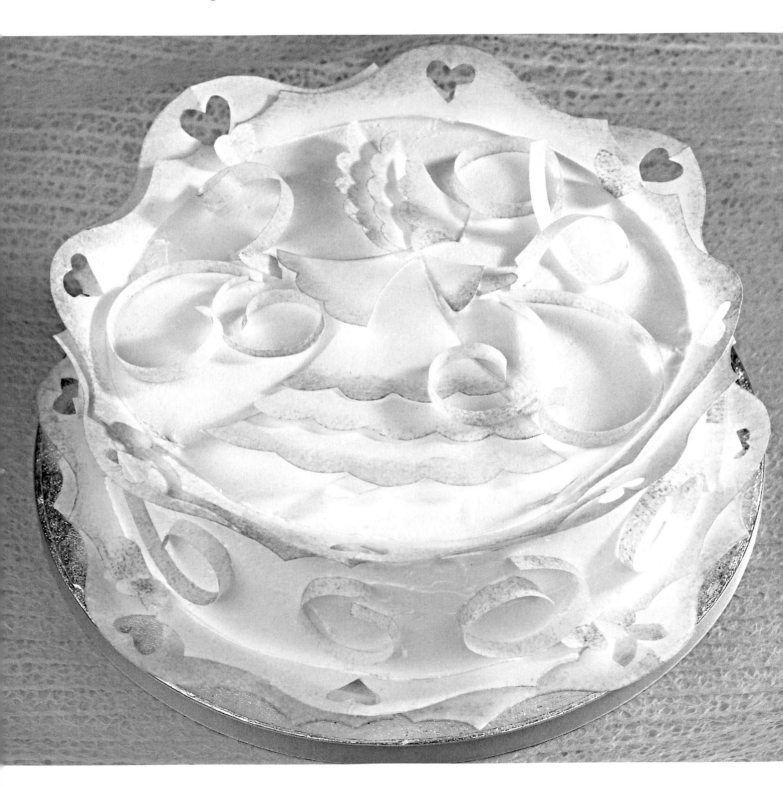

ingredients

1 pack rice paper

Edible blue and pink dusting powder

2 tbsp icing sugar

20-cm (8-in) round sponge cake (see
    page 10)

2 quantities buttercream (see page 26)

equipment

Pencil

Scissors

Saucers

Paintbrush

Carving knife

Palette knife

25-cm (10-in) round cake board

Tweezers

tips

To save time you could use just four border sections around both the top and base.

Be careful with candles on this design because the rice paper could catch fire. If you do use them, place securely in candle holders on top of the cake, away from any rice paper twirls and blow them out as soon as possible.

1 With the smooth side of the rice paper uppermost, lightly trace over the figure templates on page 31 with a pencil. Cut out just inside the pencil lines.

2 Fold a piece of rice paper in half and line the folded edge up to the edge of the border template. Trace and cut out a border. Open it out and cut out inside the pencil lines. Keep the heart shape from the middle. Make 16.

3 Tip a little blue and pink dusting powder onto a saucer. Place a little icing sugar in the centre. Using your finger, rub some dust into some icing sugar and then onto the rice paper (smooth side up). Use a light circular motion (Fig. a). Just colour along the edge of each piece of rice paper. When colouring the border sections, colour eight pink, the rest blue. Also colour all the cut out hearts and the shapes for the figure.

4 Colour two rice paper rectangles about 10 × 5cm (4 × 2in); one blue and the other pink. Cut these into thin strips. Wind the strips around a paintbrush handle to curl them (Fig. b). When finished, place all the rice paper sections to one side and prepare the cake.

5 Level the top of the cake and turn it upside-down so the base becomes the top. Slice it two or three times horizontally and fill the layers with buttercream.

6 Place the cake onto the cake board and spread buttercream around the top and sides.

7 Insert the rice paper decorations as soon as you've finished coating the cake so that they stick securely. Using the tweezers, place the main dress section in position and poke the neck section into the buttercream to hold it in place. Insert the two petticoat sections and foot beneath it. Then add the two arms and the bonnet pieces.

8 Place two blue and two pink edging sections alternatively around the edge of the cake. Position another ring of four in front of them. Repeat around the base of the cake. Place the cut-out hearts around the border so that they hide the joins.

9 Stick some of the rice paper twirls on top of the cake and the rest into the sides.

a

b

Who's looking at you? ③

The combed effect used on the sides and lid of the box make it look as though it's made of wicker. If you find the prospect of combing a bit daunting, cover the box with smooth buttercream and decorate with a few sweets instead.

ingredients

15-cm (6-in) square sponge cake (see page 10)

2 quantities vanilla buttercream (see page 26)

Blue and black food colour pastes

30g (1oz) white sugarpaste or two white marshmallows (see tips below)

15g (½oz) black sugarpaste or two chocolate buttons

equipment

Carving knife

Palette knife

20-cm (8-in) square cake board

Serrated icing comb (optional)

Piping bag (see page 96)

Star piping nozzle (optional)

15-cm (6-in) thin square cake board

Scissors

1m (36in) ribbon

techniques

Filling and covering a cake with buttercream page 27

Colouring buttercream page 26

Combing page 28

1 Level the top of the cake and turn it upside-down. Slice it horizontally two or three times. Re-assemble the cake, filling the layers with buttercream and place the cake on the board.

2 Colour about half of the buttercream pale blue. Spread a thin covering over the sides of the cake. If possible, place the cake in the fridge for about an hour.

3 Remove the cake from the fridge and spread a thicker layer of blue buttercream over the sides.

4 Holding the serrated edge of the comb vertically, run it along the sides of the cake, wiggling it slightly as you go to make the wavy pattern (Fig. a). Colour about 3 tablespoons of the buttercream black. Spread this over the top of the cake.

5 Place about 2 tablespoons of uncoloured buttercream into a piping bag fitted with the star nozzle. Pipe shells around the edges of the cake.

6 Make two white sugarpaste balls for the eyes. Stick on two black sugarpaste discs and two tiny white balls for highlights with water. Place the eyes on to the top of the cake (Fig. b).

7 To make the lid, smear pale blue buttercream over the thin cake board and use the serrated comb to make a wiggly pattern.

8 Place the lid in position on the cake and pipe around the edges.

9 To finish off, make a jaunty-looking bow and stick it on the top of the cake with a small blob of buttercream.

a

b

SUGARPASTE

Basically, sugarpaste is an edible form of modelling clay. Sometimes called fondant or ready-to-roll icing, it is simple to make and easy to use. It is also available ready-made from supermarkets and cake-decorating shops.

Recipe

There is a slight risk of salmonella from using raw egg (see note page 4). If you prefer, you can use dried egg white. Refer to the instructions on the packet for mixing it up.

ingredients

(Amounts for 1 quantity)

500g (1lb 2oz) icing sugar

1 egg white (or equivalent amount of dried egg white, reconstituted)

30ml (2 tbsp) liquid glucose (available from chemists, some
    supermarkets and cake decorating equipment shops)

1 Place the sugar into a bowl. Make a well in the centre.

2 Tip the egg white and glucose into the well and stir in using a wooden spoon.

3 Finish binding the icing together using your hands. Knead until all the sugar is incorporated and the icing feels silky and smooth.

4 Double wrap in two small plastic food bags to prevent it drying out. It can be used straightaway and does not require refrigeration. Use within a week.

Using sugarpaste

Sugarpaste will harden as it is exposed to air so if you open a packet and just use a bit, re-wrap what's leftover in a small polythene food bag to prevent it drying out. Keep unused bags of sugarpaste in a plastic container. It does not need to be kept in the fridge.

When you are rolling it out, always roll it on icing sugar never flour or cornflour. Keep a bowl of icing sugar handy to stop your fingers getting sticky. Don't worry about getting your creation "dusty" with the sugar. Simply brush marks away with a soft, damp paintbrush at the end.

When you are making models, you can use water to stick the bits together. Never soak the sugarpaste; apply just a dab with a soft paintbrush to make the surface of the sugarpaste tacky. Try to avoid getting drips of water on the sugarpaste. They will dissolve the surface, leaving an unsightly watermark behind.

QUANTITY GUIDE

The amount of sugarpaste you would use to coat a cake can vary depending upon how thick you like your icing to be. Here is a guide to give you a rough idea.

Round cake	15cm (6in)	18cm (7in)	20cm (8in)	23cm (9in)	25cm (10in)	28cm (11in)	30cm (12in)	
Square cake		15cm (6in)	18cm (7in)	20cm (8in)	23cm (9in)	25cm (10in)	28cm (11in)	30cm (12in)
Sugarpaste	500g (1lb)	650g (1lb 5oz)	800g (1lb 10oz)	900g (2lb)	1.1kg (2lb 8oz)	1.4kg (3lb)	1.6kg (3lb 8oz)	1.8kg (4lb)

Covering a cake with sugarpaste

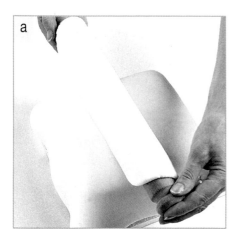
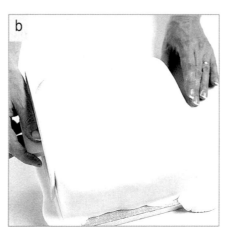
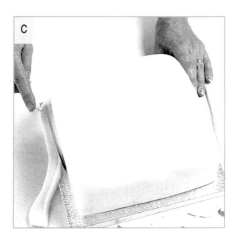

Before covering with sugarpaste, a sponge cake should be completely covered on the outside with either a coating of buttercream (see page 27) or jam. This will hold the sugarpaste in place.

If you are using a fruit cake, it should first be covered with a layer of marzipan (see page 85). When done, brush the surface of the marzipan with alcohol or cooled, boiled water. This will make it tacky so that the sugarpaste will adhere to it.

1 Dust your worksurface with icing sugar to stop the sugarpaste from sticking. Knead the sugarpaste until it feels soft and pliable.

2 Roll it out to a thickness of about 5mm (¼in). Don't roll it too thinly or it will show up any irregularities in the cake's surface.

3 Lift the sugarpaste and place over the top of the cake. You can either do this by sliding your hands – palms flat and facing upwards underneath the sugarpaste – or with a rolling pin (Fig. a).

4 Starting with the top, to try to avoid air getting trapped underneath, smooth the icing into position. A cake smoother is useful here to iron out lumps and bumps (Fig. b). If you do get an air bubble, prick it with a dressmaker's pin.

5 Cut away the excess icing from around the base (Fig. c).

BELOW *This cake is a variation on Hearts and ribbons on page 76. Cover the cake and press the heart pattern into the icing. Using about 2m (72in) of ribbon, pass it over the cake and tie under the cake board. Bring the ends back up and tie into a bow on top of the cake.*

Covering cake boards with sugarpaste

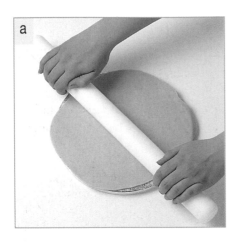

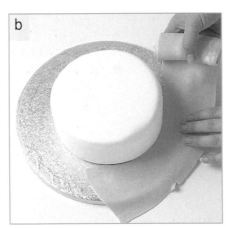

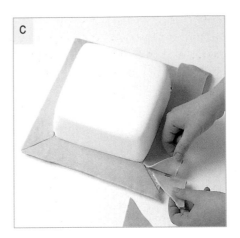

Covering the exposed cake board around the base of the cake can often neaten a design. Here are three ways of doing this.

All-in-one
This is the easiest method of covering a board.

1 Lightly moisten the entire board with water and begin to roll out a ball of sugarpaste on your work surface.

2 Lift and place the icing on to the cake board and roll it up to and over the edges of the board (Fig. a). Trim and neaten the edges. The covered cake can now be placed on top.

BELOW *The board for this cake, Frosted flowers (see page 72), was covered using the bandage method.*

The bandage method
This is done after the cake itself has been covered and is in position on the board.

1 Moisten the exposed cake board with a little water.

2 Measure the circumference of the cake and cut out a long, thin sugarpaste strip, a bit longer than that measurement and wider than the exposed board.

3 Slide a knife along under the icing to ensure that it's not stuck to the work surface and roll the icing up like a loose bandage.

4 Starting from the back, unwind the bandage around the board (Fig. b). Trim and neaten the join and edges.

Using four strips
This is a useful way to cover the board around a square or rectangular cake.

1 Moisten the cake board with a little water.

2 Thinly roll out the sugarpaste and cut out four strips each slightly longer and wider than the exposed sides of the cakeboard.

3 Lay one strip along each side of the cake. Make a diagonal cut from the edge of the board to the edge of the cake at each corner and peel away the excess icing (Fig. c).

4 The sugarpaste should now form a neat join at each corner. Trim and neaten the edges.

Colouring sugarpaste

Ready-coloured sugarpaste can be bought from cake decorating shops and some supermarkets, but it is easy to colour your own. It is best to use paste or gel colours rather than liquid ones. The pastes are thicker and won't make the icing soggy.

1 Apply dabs of food colour paste with a cocktail stick (Fig. d).

2 Knead the colour in until all of the sugarpaste is an even colour (Fig. e).

As well as using food colour, you also can knead different colours of sugarpaste together to get different shades, for example you can mix white with black to make grey. For a flat matt colour, knead until all the colour is mixed in and no streaks are visible.

Different effects with colour

Woodgrain effect

Achieving a woodgrain effect is simple and like marbling (see page 64), it can be done in two ways.

1 Roll some white sugarpaste into a sausage shape and apply some streaks of brown food colour (Fig. f) or bits of brown sugarpaste.

2 Fold the sugarpaste in half and roll it into a sausage again. Keep repeating this rolling and folding process and you will see a woodgrain effect appear (Fig. g).

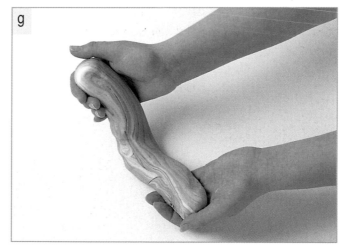

3 Stop before it becomes a solid colour and roll the sugarpaste out. If you go too far, add some bits of white sugarpaste and repeat the process.

Marbling

You can either apply a few dabs of food colour and only partially knead it in or you can use two different colours of sugarpaste. This method is shown below (Fig. a).

1 Take a lump of white sugarpaste and a smaller ball of the appropriate vein colour. Break the smaller lump into pieces and press on to the white.

2 Carefully roll and knead the two together until you see a marbled effect occurring. If you go too far and it all turns one colour, reverse the process by adding a bit more white.

3 If you are using black and white sugarpaste like this, then you can pull small bits off and roll them into balls. They make excellent icing pebbles or rocks and can even be used as candle holders.

Multicoloured effects

Another easy effect can be achieved by breaking three or four different colours of sugarpaste in to lumps, then lightly press and roll them together (Fig. b). Useful if you're putting together a groovy disco or party cake!

Painting on sugarpaste

If possible, leave the cake to harden overnight before painting on it. This will make the surface of the cake less prone to dents if you lean on it. You must only use food colours for painting.

1 Brush the surface of the cake with a pastry brush to get rid of any icing sugar which might cause the colour to bleed.

2 Paint a light outline on the cake first using some watered down food colour, then fill it in.

3 Use the food colour like watercolour paints, mixing them in a palette to get different shades (Fig. c). If you want to paint a black outline around the images, do this after you have painted the middle. If you paint the black outlines first, the black will bleed into the central colour.

4 If you make a mistake, gently dab and break up the error with a soft paintbrush dipped into clean water. Wipe away the mistake with a clean, damp cloth.

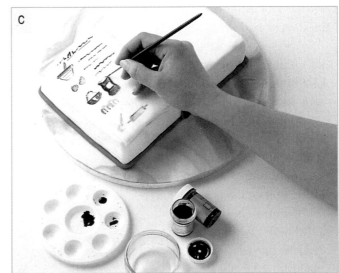

Easy sugarpaste effects

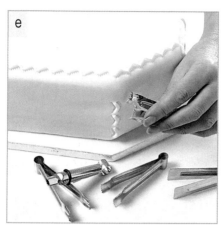

Crimping

Crimping tools are available from all cake decorating shops. Inexpensive and easy to use, they are a simple and quick way to give your sugarpaste cakes neat, decorative edges. (See the "letter A" cake on page 17 and the "number 3" cake on page 19).

1 Place the crimper on the edge of the cake, then squeeze firmly and release (Fig. d).

2 The crimper pinches the icing, leaving behind a pattern (Fig. e).

Twisting strands

If you're not keen on piping, a simple, effective edging can be made by twisting a thin sugarpaste strand and laying it around the top or base of a cake (Fig. f). Use dabs of water to hold it in place.

Quilting and embossing

A quilted effect can be made by using a ruler to press lines into the sugarpaste. You can also achieve an embossed effect by pressing things into the sugarpaste. Cake decorating shops sell decorative stamps especially designed for this, but you can also use cutters to make a similar effect (see Hearts and ribbons on page 76).

Sugarpaste cutters

There are all sorts of cutters available from cake decorating and kitchen shops which you can use to cut out a variety of patterns and shapes, including flowers and leaves.

The tiny cutters in the foreground of this picture below are called plunge cutters. They cut out tiny flower shapes. They have a small plunger inside which helps expel the flower so you can press it directly on to the cake.

Lettering

It is also possible to buy sets of alphabet cutters so you can cut out letters and stick words on to the top of your cake. You can also use letter cutters as embossers and press them into the iced cake to make words.

Modelling with sugarpaste

Simple figures

If you were to pull a sugarpaste figure apart you would see that the shapes of the components are very simple – usually a collection of cone, ball and sausage shapes (Fig. a). Make the components as you go along, otherwise the pieces may crack when you come to assemble the figure.

It is easier to make lying or sitting figures rather than standing ones. If the figure seems a bit wobbly, poke a short length of raw, dried spaghetti inside to act as a support. Use light dabs of water to stick the components of the body together.

Plaques

There are a couple of advantages to using decorated plaques on a cake. Firstly; they can be made weeks in advance. Secondly; if you are a little scared about piping a message directly on to a cake, you can pipe it on to a plaque first then place the plaque on to the cake. If you make a mistake on a plaque, it only takes minutes to make another.

1 Cut out a piece of sugarpaste to the desired shape. Leave to dry.

2 The plaque can be decorated in whatever manner you like – it can be piped, painted on or decorated with sweets.

Simple roses

Cakes decorated with sugarpaste flowers look beautiful, but they are quite tricky to make and take a lot of practise. However, simple roses are very easy to make and look effective and elegant (Fig. b). There is an even simpler rose shown on page 118, which can be made out of sugarpaste as well.

1 Make a small sugarpaste cone shape. Pinch one side to make a flap and wind around the outside of the cone.

2 Make two small, flat petals and stick around the centre, on the lower part of the petal, with dabs of water.

3 Make three more petal shapes and stick around the outside of the rose. The petals should overlap slightly. Tweak the tips of the petals and cut off any excess from the base. Cut simple leaf shapes out of green sugarpaste. Press the back of a knife into the icing to create veins.

Templates

Pretty butterflies (pages 38–39)
Hearts and ribbons (pages 76–77)

Christening cake (pages 82–83)

These templates are shown at 100%.

sugarpaste

Party balloons ❶

A versatile cake that is suitable for all sorts of happy occasions – birthdays, leaving parties, a new house, passing exams – basically any celebration.

ingredients

15-cm (6-in) round sponge cake (see page 10)

1 quantity buttercream (see page 26)

Icing sugar for rolling out

500g (1lb 2oz) white sugarpaste

30g (1oz) red sugarpaste

30g (1oz) yellow sugarpaste

30g (1oz) blue sugarpaste

30g (1oz) green sugarpaste

Black food colour

Small, round coloured chocolate sweets

equipment

Carving knife

Palette knife

20-cm (8-in) round cake board

Rolling pin

Paintbrush

Cake smoother (optional)

Small sharp knife

Piping bag (see page 96; also see tip opposite)

No. 1 piping nozzle (see tip opposite)

techniques

Filling and covering a cake with buttercream page 27

Colouring sugarpaste page 63

Covering a cake with sugarpaste page 61

1 Level the cake and turn it upside down. Slice it into two or three layers, fill the layers with buttercream and re-assemble.

2 Place the cake onto the cake board and spread buttercream around the sides and top of the cake.

3 Dust your work surface with icing sugar and knead and roll out the white sugarpaste to a thickness of about 2cm (¾in).

4 Roll each of the four sugarpaste colours into tiny balls and stick onto the white, using very light dabs of water.

5 Roll over the entire slab of icing (Fig. a). As they are pushed into the icing, the balls should lengthen and form balloon shapes.

6 Lift and place the icing over the cake. Smooth the top and sides and trim away any excess icing from around the base.

7 Colour about 1 tablespoon of buttercream black or dark grey and place into a piping bag fitted with a number 1 piping nozzle. At the bottom of each balloon, pipe two triangles to give the impression of a bow and a wiggly string (Fig. b).

8 Using buttercream, stick a line of coloured sweets around the base of the cake and place a few extra sweets on the top.

tip

If you don't want to pipe the strings on the balloons, you can paint them instead using black food colour and a fine paintbrush.

a
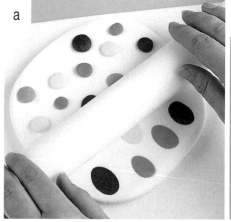

b
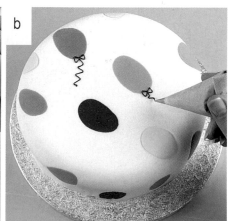

Fearsome dragon ❶

Will any daring knight or princess dare to steal the fairy cakes this fearsome dragon is guarding? I think so! Because fairy cakes are so simple to make and decorate, this is a project that children could help with.

ingredients

750g (1½lb) green sugarpaste
15g (½oz) white sugarpaste
Icing sugar for rolling out
Black food colour or black food colour pen
6–7 square biscuits or sweets
About 12 decorated fairy cakes
   (see page 10)

equipment

Approx. 30-cm (12-in) round dinner plate
   or cake board
Paintbrush
Piping nozzle (any)
Small sharp knife

techniques

Colouring sugarpaste page 63
Making fairy cakes page 10
Embossing sugarpaste page 65

a

b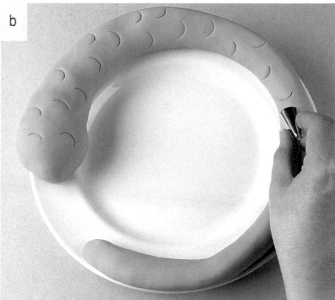

1 Begin with the dragon's body. Roll out about 600g (1¼lb) green sugarpaste into a tapering sausage shape about 65cm (25in) long (Fig. a).

2 Use dabs of water to stick the body in place around the outside edge of the plate.

3 Holding a piping nozzle at a slight angle, press it into the body to give the impression of scales (Fig. b).

4 Pull a lump off the leftover green sugarpaste and put to one side to use for the eyelids and ears later. Roll the rest into a sausage shape for the head. Squeeze the middle so that it goes in and stick the head against the thickest part of the body (Fig. a). Add scales.

5 Use the back of a knife to press a line around the front of the head for a mouth and the end of a paintbrush to press two holes for the nostrils.

6 To make the eyes, make two tiny white sugarpaste almond shapes. Stick them onto the face with water. Make two tiny green sugarpaste string shapes for eyebrows and stick over the eyes.

7 Make two tiny green carrot shapes for ears and stick onto the head. Press a paintbrush handle into each one to give a bit of definition.

8 Paint two black dots on the eyes with black food colour and a paintbrush or with a black food colour pen.

9 Cut about six square biscuits or sweets in half diagonally and press into the dragon's back to make his spikes. Use one to make the point on his tail.

10 Fill the centre of the plate with decorated fairy cakes.

variation

This dinosaur is made in exactly the same way as the dragon except that once the icing had been rolled into a head shape, the back of the head was pulled and pinched to form a frill shape and it doesn't have any spikes.

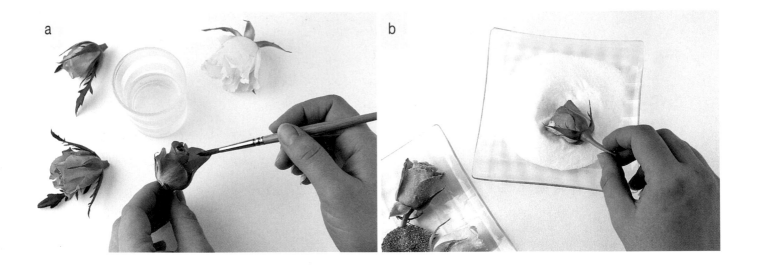

a

b

Frosted flowers ❶

A design so simple, there's virtually no decorating involved! You can frost other flowers such as freesias, pansies, petunias, primulas and violets. If you choose flowers other than these, you must make sure that they are not poisonous. With deep red roses and a red or dark green ribbon, this would also make a stunning Christmas cake.

ingredients

20-cm (8-in) round sponge cake (see page 10)

1 quantity buttercream (see page 26)

Icing sugar, for rolling out

1kg (2lb) white or ivory sugarpaste

1 egg white or 5 tbsp caster sugar dissolved in 1 tbsp hot, boiled water

125g (4oz) caster sugar

equipment

Carving knife

Palette knife

25-cm (10-in) round cake board

Rolling pin

Cake smoother (optional)

Small sharp knife

Soft paintbrush

6–8 rose blooms (washed, dried and stems cut off)

Saucer

10–12 rose leaves (washed and dried)

70cm (28in) pink ribbon, 4cm (1½in) wide

Adhesive tape

techniques

Filling and covering a cake with buttercream page 27

Covering a cake with sugarpaste page 61

Covering a cakeboard page 62

Using ribbon page 24

1 Level the top of the cake and turn it upside down so that the flat base now forms the top of the cake. Slice the cake horizontally into two or three layers, fill the layers with buttercream and re-assemble.

2 Place the cake on the cake board and spread a thin covering of buttercream around the top and sides. Place to one side.

3 Dust your work surface with icing sugar and knead the sugarpaste until pliable. Roll it out and lift and place over the cake. Smooth the top and sides and trim away the excess from around the base.

4 Pick out any crumbs from the leftover icing and use it to cover the cake board using the bandage method (see page 62).

5 Using a soft paintbrush, dab egg white or sugar solution around the tips of one of the rose blooms (Fig. a).

6 Dip the rose into a saucer of caster sugar. Shake off the excess and leave to dry (Fig. b).

7 When dry, arrange the roses and leaves on top of the cake. Place the ribbon around the base of the cake. Cut to size and use a small piece of adhesive tape to secure it at the back.

variation

This version uses silk flowers, so it's ideal for that last minute cake panic.

Scary Halloween cake ❶

Marbling is an easy effect to achieve and the ghoulish, red-veined eyeballs are also simple to make. You should be able to find jelly snake sweets easily, but if you can't, roll balls of sugarpaste into snakes instead.

sugarpaste

ingredients

15-cm (6-in) round sponge cake (see
    page 10)
1 quantity buttercream (see page 26)
500g (1lb 2oz) white sugarpaste
Icing sugar, for rolling out
30g (1oz) black sugarpaste
Red food colour paste
7–8 jelly snakes
Black food colour paste or black food
    colour pen

equipment

Carving knife
Palette knife
25-cm (10-in) round cake board
Rolling pin
Cake smoother (optional)
Small sharp knife
Fine and medium paintbrushes

techniques

Filling and covering a cake with
    buttercream page 27
Marbling sugarpaste page 64
Covering a cake with sugarpaste page 61
Painting on sugarpaste page 64

1 Level the top of the cake and turn it upside down. Slice it two or three times horizontally and sandwich the layers together with buttercream. Place the cake on the board and spread buttercream around the sides and top.

2 Pull off a 90g (3oz) lump of white sugarpaste and place to one side. Dust your work surface with icing sugar and knead the remaining white icing until soft.

3 Tear 20g (¾oz) of the black sugarpaste into bits and press into the white. Roll the two colours into a thick sausage shape. Fold the sausage in half and re-roll. Repeat another two or three times, then roll out (Fig. a).

4 Lift and place the icing on top of the cake and smooth the top and sides. Trim away any excess from around the base.

5 Pull a little bit off the white sugarpaste you set aside at the beginning. Put this to one side for making highlights and snake eyes later. Roll the rest into three ball shapes for the eyeballs.

6 Divide the leftover black sugarpaste into three and roll into three balls. Flatten the balls into discs and stick one on to each eye with a dab of water.

7 Make three tiny flat white discs and stick one on to each eye for highlights.

8 Paint blood vessels on to the eyes using red food colour and a fine paintbrush (Fig. b). Stick the eyeballs in place on top of the cake with dabs of water.

9 Arrange the snakes around the top of the cake and the board. If they won't stay in place, stick them with little dabs of water.

10 Make two tiny white sugarpaste balls for eyes for each snake and stick on with water. Using either a black food colour pen or black food colour and a fine paintbrush, add tiny black food colour dots for pupils.

tip

For a really ghoulish surprise, you could colour the cake mixture green before baking and fill with orange or purple coloured buttercream.

a
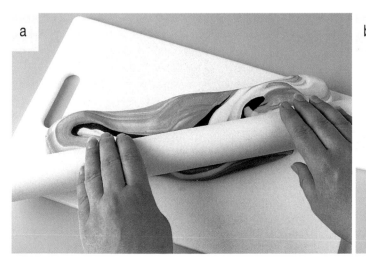

b
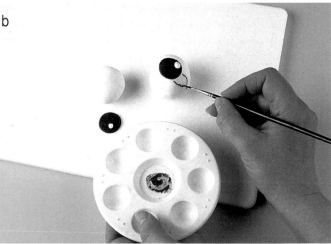

Hearts and ribbons ❷

A stylish idea for Valentine's day or an anniversary. Ribbon insertion is a traditional form of cake decorating. Here, wide ribbon gives the cake a more contemporary feel. A variation of this cake is shown on page 61.

ingredients

18-cm (7-in) square sponge cake (see page 10)
1 quantity buttercream (see page 26)
Icing sugar, for rolling out
750g (1½lb) white sugarpaste
200g (6½oz) red sugarpaste
2 tbsp white royal icing (optional; see tip opposite)

equipment

Greaseproof or tracing paper
Pencil
Scissors
Carving knife
Palette knife
25-cm (10-in) round cake board
Rolling pin
Cake smoother (optional)
Small sharp knife
Heart-shaped cutter
Piping bag
No. 3 piping nozzle (optional; see tip opposite)
Scalpel or small, sharp knife
1m (36in) ribbon
Paintbrush

techniques

Filling and covering a cake with buttercream page 27
Covering a cake with sugarpaste page 61
Embossing a pattern page 65
Covering a board with sugarpaste page 62
Piping page 98

1 Trace the heart template on page 67. Cut out. Place the template on the cake and cut round it (see Fig. b on page 39).

2 Split the cake into two or three layers and re-assemble, sandwiching the layers together with buttercream. Place cake on board. Spread a thin coating of buttercream over the sides and top of the cake.

3 Dust your work surface with icing sugar and roll out the white sugarpaste to a thickness of about 1cm (½in). Lift and place onto the cake and smooth the icing into position. Trim away the excess from around the base.

4 Gently press a heart-shaped cutter into the icing to leave an impression of the shape (Fig. a). Try not to go right through the icing or there's a chance the buttercream might ooze out. Repeat all over the cake.

5 Moisten the exposed cake board with a little water. Thinly roll out the red sugarpaste. Cut it into strips and lay it around the base of the cake so that it covers the board. Trim and neaten the edges (Fig. b).

6 Place about 1 tablespoon of white royal icing into a piping bag fitted with a number 3 piping nozzle and pipe a "snail trail" (see page 98) around the base of the cake.

7 Using a scalpel or an extremely sharp knife, cut two slits the same length as the width of your ribbon about 2.5cm (1in) apart on the side of the cake.

8 Cut about 5 cm (2 in) of ribbon. Insert the ends into the slits (Fig. c). Use the scalpel to poke the ribbon in securely. Repeat two or three times over the cake.

9 Make a bow with the remaining ribbon and stick on top of the cake using either a dab of royal icing or a moistened ball of white sugarpaste.

10 Brush away any dusty fingerprints from the board with a soft damp paintbrush.

tips

Don't want to pipe around the base of the cake? Stick small white sugarpaste balls around it instead.

Because of the amount of fabric on this design it is not advisable to use candles.

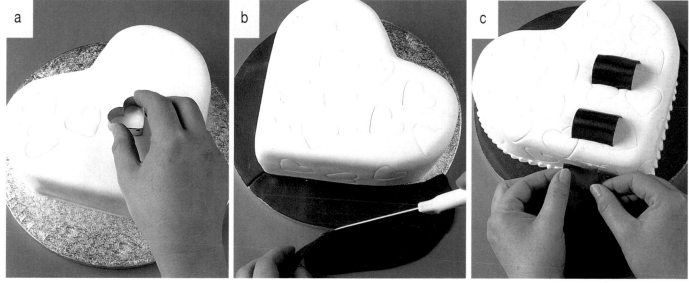

a

b

c

Christmas parcel ❷

The technique shown here is a simple form of marquetry. Icing shapes are cut out and replaced with others of an identical shape but in a different colour. Despite being a Christmas design, it is not obligatory to use fruitcake. Substitute sponge cake and buttercream and omit the marzipan if you prefer.

ingredients

15-cm (6-in) square fruit cake (see page 14)
3 tbsp brandy (optional)
3 tbsp boiled apricot jam
Icing sugar, for rolling out
500g (1lb 2oz) marzipan
500g (1lb 2oz) white sugarpaste
250g (8oz) green sugarpaste
45g (1½oz) red sugarpaste

equipment

Carving knife
20-cm (8-in) square cake board
Cocktail stick
Pastry brush
Rolling pin
Cake smoother (optional)
Small sharp knife
Holly leaf cutter
1m (36in) ribbon
Scissors

techniques

Covering a fruit cake with marzipan page 85
Covering a cake with sugarpaste page 61

1 Level the top of the cake and turn it upside-down on the cake board. Pierce the top of the cake a few times with the cocktail stick and drizzle the brandy over the top. Brush the apricot jam over the top and sides of the cake.

2 Dust your work surface with icing sugar. Knead and roll out the marzipan. Lay the marzipan over the top of the cake and smooth the top and sides. Trim any excess from around the base.

3 Place a few light dabs of water on the surface of the marzipan. These are just to hold the sugarpaste covering in place. If you soak the marzipan you will not be able to remove the sugarpaste cutouts, so use a light hand.

4 Sprinkle more icing sugar on your work surface and knead and roll out the white sugarpaste. Lift and place over the cake. Smooth the top and sides and neaten around the base as before.

5 Press the holly leaf cutter into the cake. Try to just cut through the sugarpaste and not the marzipan or the cake. Remove the leaf shape (Fig. a). Cut out leaf shapes all over the cake.

6 Roll out the green sugarpaste. Try to make it roughly the same thickness as the white sugarpaste cake covering.

7 Using the holly leaf cutter, cut out enough green leaves to replace the white ones you have cut out of the cake. Re-roll the leftover green sugarpaste as necessary.

8 Place the leaves into the gaps on the cake using dabs of water (Fig. b). Using the back of a knife, press a few lines into each leaf for veins.

9 Make tiny red sugarpaste balls for berries. Squash them and stick on to the cake with water.

10 To tie the ribbon, pass both ends under the cake board and tie in a knot. Bring the ends back up and tie into a bow. Trim the ends if necessary to neaten them.

tips

By using different cutters, you could easily adapt this design to suit any occasion. For example, use a flower cutter and pink sugarpaste to make a pretty birthday parcel.

You could make a rectangular sugarpaste label and pipe a message on it.

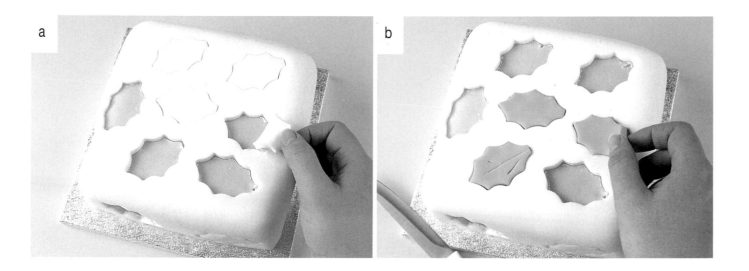

Happy gardener ❸

Brown sugar makes incredibly realistic looking soil. However, it is very crunchy. For a softer alternative, dab chocolate buttercream around the top and base of the cake instead.

ingredients

20-cm (8-in) square sponge cake (see page 10)
1 quantity buttercream (see page 26)
Icing sugar for rolling out
800g (1lb 12oz) cream coloured sugarpaste
75g (2½oz) brown sugarpaste
Black food colour
300g (11oz) green sugarpaste
1 strand raw, dried spaghetti
100g (4oz) flesh/terracotta-coloured sugarpaste (use "paprika" food colour paste or a mixture of pink, yellow and white sugarpaste)
Silver food colour (optional; see tip)
45g (1½oz) brown sugar

equipment

Carving knife
Palette knife
25-cm (10-in) square cake board
Rolling pin
Cake smoother (optional)
Small, sharp knife
Paintbrush
Piping nozzle (any)

1 Level the top of the cake and turn it over so that the base now forms the top. Slice the cake horizontally into two or three layers and then sandwiching the layers back together with buttercream. Place the cake onto the board and thinly coat the sides and top of the cake with buttercream.

2 Dust your work surface with icing sugar. Knead the cream coloured sugarpaste until pliable and roll it out to a thickness of about 1cm (⅓in). Lift and place over the cake. Smooth the top and sides and trim away the excess with a sharp knife.

3 To make the gardener, roll 60g (2oz) brown sugarpaste into a sausage shape, 18cm (7in) long. Bend it into a horseshoe shape (Fig. a). Slice the ends off and stick in the centre of the cake with a dab of water.

4 Knead a little black food colour into about 150g (5oz) of green sugarpaste to make a khaki colour. Roll about 90g (3oz) into a conical shape for his body. Flatten the base and top slightly and stick on top of the legs with a little water.

5 To stop the man falling over, stick a strand of spaghetti into the body. Leave a bit protruding for the head.

6 Roll about 30g (1oz) flesh-coloured sugarpaste into a ball for the man's head. Stick it on top of the body (Fig. b). Poke the edge of a piping nozzle into the lower part of the face to make a smile.

7 Make three tiny flesh-coloured ball shapes. Use these for the ears and nose and stick them in position. Poke a hollow into each ear with the end of a paintbrush.

8 Roll 10g (⅓oz) khaki green sugarpaste into a ball and flatten it to make the cap. Stick on top of his head and press a line into the front of the cap with the back of a knife.

9 Roll about 20g (¾oz) khaki green sugarpaste into a sausage. Cut it in half to make his arms. Stick one either side of his body.

10 For the boots, make two 15g (½oz) khaki green sausages. Bend into "L" shapes and stick on to the legs. Press four lines into the sole of each boot with the back of a knife.

11 To make a flowerpot, roll 15g (½oz) flesh-coloured sugarpaste into a conical shape. Flatten the base and top. Roll and cut out a long thin flesh-coloured strip and stick around the top of the pot (Fig. c). Make three pots and stick around the man. Paint a black food colour dot on the base of each pot.

12 Make two sugarpaste balls for the man's hands; flatten slightly. Stick one on the end of each arm, one resting on top of a flowerpot.

13 To make a spade, roll 10g (⅓oz) brown sugarpaste into a long string. Cut a small section off the end and lay across the top of the longer section to form a "T" shape. Stick on to the cake and add a square cream piece for the blade.

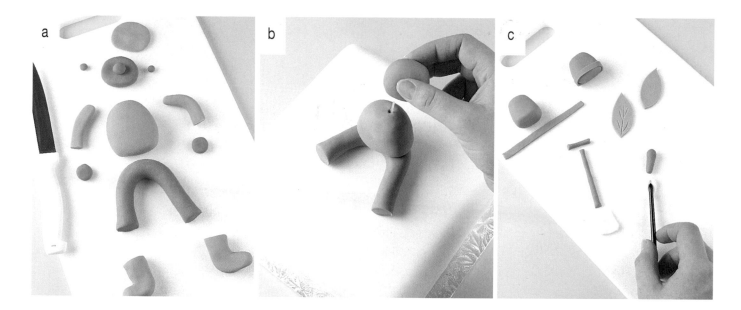

a

b

c

14 For the trowel, roll a tiny bit of brown sugarpaste into a pellet shape for the handle. Make a similar cream shape for the blade. Press a paintbrush handle into the blade to give it a curved shape. Stick onto the cake.

15 Paint the relevant bits of the trowel and spade silver, with food colour.

16 Use the remaining green sugarpaste to make the leaves. Roll it out thinly and cut out simple leaf shapes. Press a couple of veins into each leaf with the back of a knife, put a dab of water onto the back of each leaf and stick them around the sides of the cake.

17 To finish, moisten the top of the cake with a little water and carefully spoon the sugar around the character. Do the same around the leaves on the cake board.

tip

If you cannot get silver food colour, use grey sugarpaste to make the trowel and spade blades instead.

Christening cake ❸

At first glance, this may look like a terribly complicated cake to attempt but it isn't as tricky as it looks. You can take your time over it. The top plaque with the bootees can be made weeks in advance. This pretty broderie anglaise technique works just as well in blue (see Baby's cradle on page 108).

ingredients

20-cm (8-in) square sponge cake (see page 10)
1 quantity buttercream (see page 26)
Icing sugar, for rolling out
1kg (2lb 4oz) white sugarpaste
500g (1lb 2oz) pink sugarpaste
1 quantity royal icing (see page 90)
Pink food colour

equipment

Carving knife
Palette knife
30-cm (12-in) square cake board
Rolling pin
Cake smoother (optional)
Small, sharp knife
Paintbrush
3 piping bags (see page 96)
No. 1 and star piping nozzles
Greaseproof or tracing paper
Pencil
Scissors
1m (36in) thin, pink ribbon

techniques

Filling and covering a cake with buttercream page 27
Covering a cake with sugarpaste page 61
Covering a cakeboard with sugarpaste page 62
Piping page 98

1 To prepare the cake, level the top and turn it upside down. Slice it horizontally into two or three layers, fill with buttercream and re-assemble. Place it in the centre of the cake board and spread butter-cream around the sides and top.

2 Dust your work surface with icing sugar and knead and roll out 800g (1lb 10oz) white sugarpaste. Lift and place over the cake. Smooth the top and sides and trim and neaten around the base.

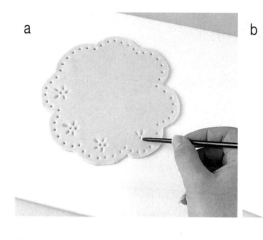

a

b

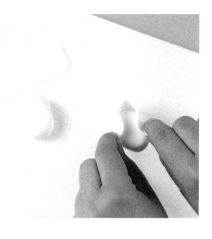

c

3 Lightly moisten the visible cake board and thinly roll out about 350g (12oz) pink sugarpaste. Cut into four strips and use it to cover the cake board (see page 62). Trim and neaten the edges.

4 Using a paintbrush handle, press a series of dots and dashes into the pink icing to form a pattern. The centre of a flower is a dot and a series of six dashes around the outside form the petals (refer to Fig. a). Place about 3 tablespoons of white royal icing into a piping bag fitted with a star nozzle and pipe a "snail trail" around the base of the cake.

5 To make the plaque, roll out another 150g (5oz) pink sugarpaste. Trace the template on page 67 and cut out. Place the template onto the pink sugarpaste and cut out the flower shape. Using the paintbrush, press a line of dots around the outside of the shape and a circle of dot and dash flowers just inside (Fig. a).

6 Place about 1 tablespoon of white royal icing into a piping bag fitted with a number 1 piping nozzle. Carefully pipe around the outside of all the dots and dashes on both the board and the plaque (Fig. b).

7 Place a few dabs of water on top of the cake. Using a palette knife, carefully lift and place the plaque into position.

8 To make the bootees, make two 15g (½oz) white sugarpaste balls. Squash both into flattish oval shapes. Take another two 15g (½oz) lumps of white and roll out. Cut out two rectangles about 12cm (5in) long. Round the corners of the rectangles slightly.

9 Fold a rectangle around the top of an oval to form a bootee (Fig. c). Poke a few lace holes with the end of a paintbrush. Repeat with the second bootee, then stick them in place on the plaque with a light dab of water.

10 Colour about 2 tablespoons of royal icing pink and place in a piping bag with a number 1 piping nozzle. Pipe a couple of lines on each bootee to make the laces.

11 Pipe a zigzag pattern around the edges of the plaque to hide any rough edges.

12 Pipe a small floral pattern on each of the four corners of the cake using a series of dots and dashes.

13 Make four tiny pink ribbon bows and stick in position with royal icing dots.

tip

When using a fine piping nozzle, it helps if you make the icing slightly runnier than usual by stirring in a few drops of water.

variation

A plaque this shape suits all sorts of other shaped cakes as well. Here the plaque has been decorated more intricately. You could pipe the baby's name in the centre if you wish.

MARZIPAN

Made out of ground almonds, the difference between marzipan and almond paste is that marzipan contains a higher proportion of almonds so is usually a little more expensive. The taste is very similar and they behave the same way when working with them. You can make your own marzipan or you can buy it. It is readily available from shops in two shades; the traditional yellow (labelled "gold") or white. It can be coloured using food colour so could be used instead of sugarpaste on most of the designs on pages 68–83.

Recipe

This recipe lightly cooks the eggs and produces a marzipan that is fairly firm and not too oily. (If you are concerned about the eggs being only lightly cooked, see page 4, use ready-made marzipan instead.)

ingredients

1 whole egg and one egg yolk
110g (4oz) caster sugar
110g (4oz) icing sugar (sieved)
225g (8oz) ground almonds
A few drops of almond essence

1 Put the eggs and sugars into a heatproof bowl and place over a pan of hot water. Whisk until thick and creamy.

2 Remove the bowl from the heat and add a few drops of almond essence. Using a wooden spoon, stir in the ground almonds then lightly knead into a ball. The marzipan will firm up slightly as it cools, but if you feel it is still too soft, add a little more icing sugar.

STORING: Ideally this should be used as soon as possible but if you have to store it for a day or so, double-wrap it in a small plastic bag or cling film and keep in the refrigerator. Use within a week.

TIP If the marzipan is hard to knead, microwave it for 10–15 seconds. Test it and repeat if necessary. Don't overdo it as the oils in the centre can burn.

ABOVE *Marzipan shapes are quick and easy to make.*

QUANTITY GUIDE

Although amounts will vary depending upon how thick you like your marzipan, here is a rough guide to the quantities you require to cover different sized cakes.

Round cake	15cm (6in)	18cm (7in)	20cm (8in)	23cm (9in)	25cm (10in)	28cm (11in)	30cm (12in)	
Square cake		15cm (6in)	18cm (7in)	20cm (8in)	23cm (9in)	25cm (10in)	28cm (11in)	30cm (12in)
Marzipan	500g (1lb)	650g (1lb 5oz)	800g (1lb 10oz)	900g (2lb)	1.1kg (2lb 8oz)	1.4kg (3lb)	1.6kg (3lb 8oz)	1.8kg (4lb)

Covering a fruit cake for sugarpaste or swirled royal icing

Because razor sharp edges are not required for sugarpaste or swirled royal icing, the whole cake can be covered in one go.

1 Place the cake in position on the board. If the top is slightly domed, slice this off and place the cake upside down on the board. Plug any holes left by currants with small balls of marzipan. If you want to, drizzle a little brandy over the top of the cake and allow it to sink in. Heat some apricot jam in a small saucepan or in a bowl in the microwave to boiling point and brush over the top and sides of the cake. Knead the marzipan. Dust your work surface with icing sugar and roll it out (Fig. a).

2 Carefully lift the marzipan and place it on the cake (Fig. b).

3 Ease it over the top and sides of the cake and gently press into position. Trim away the excess from around the base (Fig. c).

4 Smooth over the top and sides with the flat of your hands. Ideally then use a cake smoother (Fig. d).

a

b

c

d

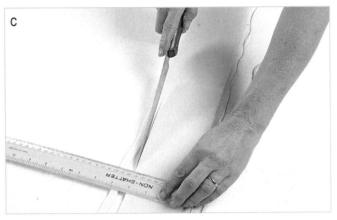

1 If the top of the cake is rounded, level it so that it is flat and turn the cake over. Fill any holes with small balls of marzipan. Drizzle a little brandy over the cake if you wish and allow it to sink in. Heat some apricot jam in a small saucepan or in a bowl in the microwave to boiling point and brush over the top of the cake (Fig. a).

2 Knead about two thirds of the marzipan and roll it out to no less than 5mm (¼ in) thickness. Place the cake upside down on the marzipan and cut around the edge (Fig. b).

3 Turn the cake the right way up and place on the board. Measure the circumference of the cake and make a note of the measurement. Spread jam around the sides. Knead and roll out the rest of the marzipan (including the trimmings). Cut a strip the same length as the circumference of the cake and as wide as the height of the cake, including the marzipan topping (Fig. c).

4 Roll the marzipan strip up like a bandage and unwind it around the sides of the cake (Fig. d).

5 Leave to dry for at least 48 hours before icing. It is important that the surfaces, edges and corners of the marzipan are smooth and sharp, as any crinkle or bump will show through the royal icing.

Covering a square fruit cake for smooth royal icing

1 Level the top of the cake if necessary and brush it with boiled apricot jam (Fig. a).

2 Knead about two thirds of the marzipan and roll it out to no less than 5mm (¼ in) thickness. Place the cake, upside down on the marzipan. Trim around the cake (Fig. b) and place the right way up on the board.

3 Measure the length and width of one side of the cake. Cut four strips of marzipan using those measurements (Fig. c).

4 Spread jam over the sides and stick the strips of marzipan onto the cake (Fig. d).

5 Leave the cake to dry for at least 48 hours before icing. Make sure that all of the surfaces, edges and corners are as smooth and sharp as possible.

a

b

c

d

Colouring marzipan

It is easy to colour marzipan. Simply add colour (paste or gel colours work best as they're less likely to make the marzipan soggy) and knead in. Because gold marzipan is already quite a strong colour, it will distort some colours such as blue and give them a greenish tint. Therefore, if you're planning to colour marzipan, it's best to use the white variety.

1 Apply the colour to the marzipan with a cocktail stick (Fig. a).

2 Knead the colour into the marzipan, ensuring that it is evenly blended (Fig. b).

Modelling with marzipan

The principles of modelling with marzipan are the same as those for sugarpaste (see pages 66). You can make models of virtually anything – people, animals, flowers etc. Use water to stick the pieces of marzipan together.

Little fruits like these are fun and easy to make. They could be used as cake decorations or even as sweet treats at Christmas. The blush on the apple was made by brushing a little edible dusting powder over the green. You could achieve a similar effect by dabbing a little red food colour on the apple instead.

ABOVE *On this design, nuts were arranged on top of the fruit cake before baking and glazed with boiled apricot jam when the cake had cooled. A pattern of simple marzipan santas stand around the edges. You could use stars if you prefer.*

RIGHT *Marzipan fruits are a very simple way to create a beautifully decorated cake. The edge is simply crimped (see page 65) and the cake and board trimmed with a yellow ribbon.*

ROYAL ICING

Royal icing is extremely versatile. Made from egg whites and icing sugar, it can be used for both covering and piping cakes. It has a more crisp texture than sugarpaste and gives a cake a very classic, polished look. It sets hard, so can be used to create all sorts of extravagant effects. When using royal icing it is important that all of your bowls and utensils are dry and grease-free, so give them a wash in hot soapy water before you start. It may take a few attempts to perfect your technique with royal icing, but the finished result is worth the effort.

Recipe

If you are using royal icing to coat a cake, it is essential that you include glycerine and lemon juice. The glycerine enables you to get a knife cleanly through the icing when you cut the cake and the lemon juice keeps the icing white.

If you are just making icing to pipe flowers, snail trail round a cake or to make the runouts on the Snowflakes (see pages 112–113) and Baby's cradle (see pages 108–109) cakes you can leave these two items out.

There is a slight risk of salmonella from using raw egg (see note page 4). If you prefer, you can used dried egg white substitute; refer to the instructions on the packet.

ingredients
(Amounts for 1 quantity)

2 egg whites (or equivalent amount of dried egg white, reconstituted)

450g (1lb) icing sugar, sieved

5ml (1 tsp) lemon juice

5ml (1 tsp) glycerine

1 Reconstitute the egg white following the instructions on the packet. This normally means adding a couple of teaspoons of water and mixing it to a smooth paste. Add the rest of the water gradually, beating well until light and frothy.

2 Stir in about a quarter of the icing sugar. If using a food mixer, set it to the slowest speed.

3 Gradually add the rest of the sugar, the lemon juice and glycerine.

4 Beat until the icing stands up in peaks. If you're using a food mixer, beat on slow speed for 5 minutes. Don't be tempted to race ahead on a fast speed or your icing will be too full of air bubbles to use properly.

STORING: When the icing is ready, transfer to a clean, grease-free plastic food container with a tight fitting lid. Lay a sheet of cling film directly on top of the icing to prevent it drying out and place the lid back on the container. Always keep the icing covered when not in use and use within a week.

USING: If you have stored the icing, you need to remix it before using. Take a few tablespoons of icing out of the container and place in a small bowl. Beat it thoroughly with a knife to get rid of air bubbles and to make it nice and smooth. If you want to stop the leftover beaten icing from hardening, place a damp cloth over the top of the bowl.

Quantity guide

It is difficult to give even a rough guide for this as it really depends on how thick you want your covering of icing to be. If you have a lot of cakes to cover it is best to make up double the amount shown in the recipe and use that up before making another batch.

Colouring royal icing

It is possible to use either liquid or paste colours. If using liquid colour, don't add too much as you could overthin the icing and make it too runny to hold its shape when piping. If you are trying to achieve a pale colour, note that the icing will darken slightly as it dries.

1 Add the colour sparingly to the icing (Fig. a).

2 Mix until the icing is evenly coloured (Fig. b). If you want to keep excess icing useable in case you need more, lay a damp cloth over the top of the bowl.

Peaked and swirled effects

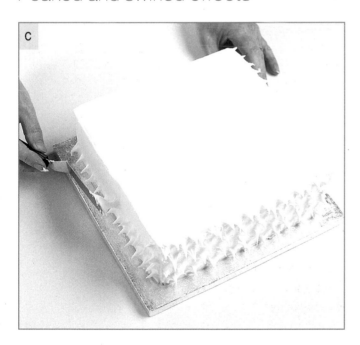

These are the easiest finishes to achieve on a royal iced cake as you don't have to be precise at all.

To get peaks in the icing, simply spread royal icing over the cake, press the palette knife into the icing and pull away sharply to leave a peak (Fig. c).

A swirly effect is achieved by simply swirling the icing about the cake as you cover it (Fig. d). This effect was used on Christmas bows (above and pages 102–103).

Royal-icing a square fruit cake

This technique is only used on a fruit cake which has been covered with marzipan, never on sponge. You will need a "straight edge" which is like a metal ruler but has no markings on it and also a cake scraper to produce a smooth finish. It will take about a week to coat the cake because the icing has to dry between layers.

1 Spread some icing over the top of the cake with a palette knife. Spread it back and forth a few times to get rid of any air bubbles, then spread it over the whole of the top of the cake. Cover the surface as evenly as possible (Fig. a).

2 Remove the excess icing from around the edges (Fig. b).

3 Take the straight edge and place it at the far end of the cake. Pull it towards you in one continuous movement (Fig. c). You should be left with a thin covering over the cake.

4 Remove the excess icing from around the edges (Fig. d) and leave the cake to dry for a minimum of three hours, preferably overnight .

5 Spread icing over one side of the cake (Fig. e).

6 Remove the excess icing from the top edge and the corners (Fig. f).

7 Stand the cake scraper at the far end of the cake and pull it towards you in one movement (Fig. g).

8 Remove the excess icing from the top edge and corners again (Fig. h). Leave to dry for another couple of hours.

9 Cover the other sides in the same way then leave the cake to dry overnight (Fig. i).

10 Ice the cake with another two layers allowing drying time between coats.

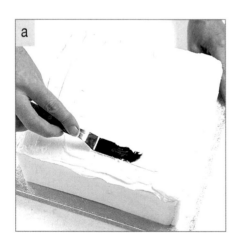

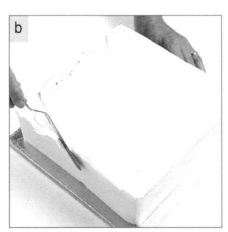

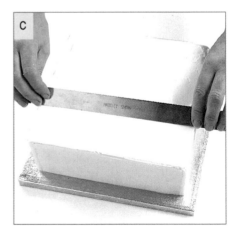

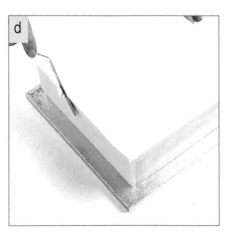

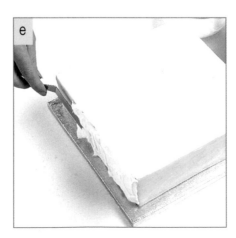

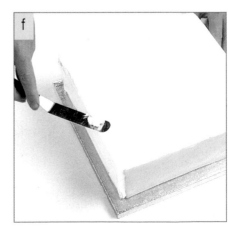

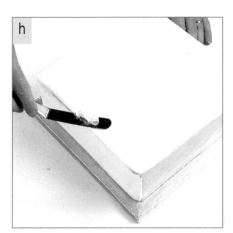

Covering a square cake board

Make sure that the royal iced cake is completely dry before putting it on a board, otherwise you may damage its finish.

1 Spread a thin layer of royal icing over one side of the board. Remove the excess icing from the edge (Fig. j).

2 Pull the cake scraper over the icing towards you in one movement (Fig. k).

3 Remove the excess from the edges (Fig. l) and repeat on the opposite side. Leave to dry for at least 3 hours and cover the other two sides. Repeat with a second layer for a neat finish.

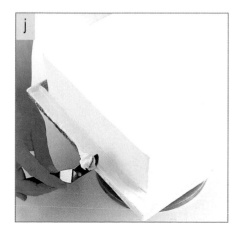

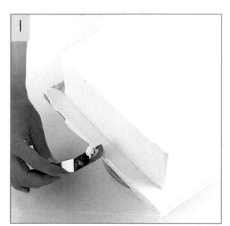

Royal-icing a round fruit cake

As well as a straight edge and cake scraper, you will need an icing turntable. This technique is only used on a fruit cake which has been covered with marzipan, never on sponge. You need to allow a week to do this, as the icing has to dry between layers.

1 Cover the top surface of the cake in the same way as described for the square cake (see page 92) and leave to dry overnight (Fig. a).

2 Spread royal icing around the sides of the cake (Fig. b).

3 Remove the excess icing from around the top edge with a palette knife (Fig. c).

4 Place the cake on the turntable. Hold the cake scraper vertically at the back of the cake; hold the board and turntable with your other hand. Turn the turntable in one revolution, pulling the scraper towards you (Fig. d). Lift the scraper off the cake (this will leave a mark).

5 Neaten the top edge again (Fig. e). Leave the cake to dry overnight. Repeat the process, building up at least three layers.

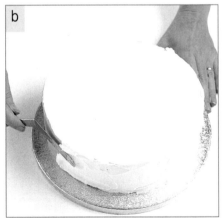

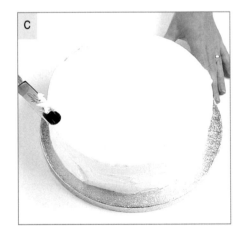

Covering a round cake board

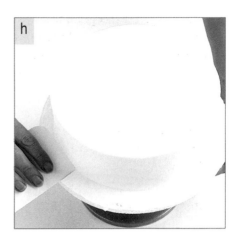

1. Stand the cake on a turntable. Spread a thin, even layer of royal icing around the board (Fig. f).

2. Remove the excess from the edges using a palette knife (Fig. g).

3. Run the cake scraper around the cake board in one continuous fluid motion (Fig. h).

4. Remove the excess from the edges again (Fig. i) and leave to dry for at least 3 hours. Repeat with a second coat.

Piping

The thought of piping can be a bit terrifying. However, if you have the right equipment and a bit of time to practise, anyone can learn some simple techniques.

There are a number of different piping sets available, from shiny syringe-type contraptions through to the humble bit of folded greaseproof paper. It is even possible to buy tubes of ready-made piping icing from the supermarket that come with a set of different nozzles that you screw on to the end. There is no right or wrong piece of equipment, use whatever suits you.

Piping bags

WASHABLE POLYESTER PIPING BAGS These have certain advantages. Obviously, because they're washable they're reusable. They don't split and burst at inopportune moments and grease from buttercream doesn't seep through the sides. They are used with a connector to which you attach the piping nozzle. This means you can change the piping nozzle without having to set up a new bag. They're also handy for making meringues.

DISPOSABLE SHOP-BOUGHT BAGS These are very convenient as they're already made up for you. There's no need to wash them after you've finished icing, you can just throw them away. Their only disadvantage is their expense.

HOMEMADE GREASEPROOF PAPER PIPING BAGS Definitely the cheapest option, as you can make hundreds of piping bags from one roll of greaseproof paper. They are quite easy to make; see the instructions opposite.

BELOW *Piping equipment can be as simple and cheap as a homemade piping bag or as easy as shop-bought tubes of ready-made icing.*

ABOVE *This pretty cradle is made entirely out of piped royal icing (see pages 108–109).*

Making a piping bag

1 Cut some greaseproof paper into a triangle.

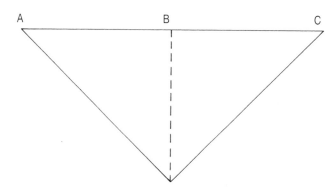

2 Pick up corner "C" and fold over, so that "B" forms a sharp cone in the centre.

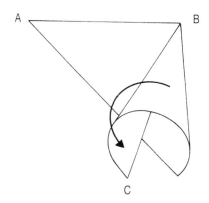

3 Wrap corner "A" around the cone.

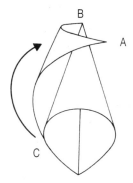

4 Make sure that "A" and "C" are at the back and that the point of the cone is sharp.

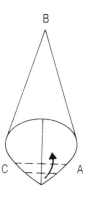 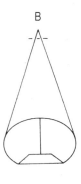

5 Fold points "A" and "C" inside the top edge of the bag to hold it securely. Snip off the end "B" and insert a nozzle.

Filling a piping bag

Usually you pipe with a piping nozzle in the end of the bag. If using a disposable or greaseproof paper bag, snip about 12mm (½in) off the end of the bag and drop a piping nozzle inside.

1 Scoop up some icing on a palette knife and place it inside the bag. Holding the knife through the bag, pull the knife out (Fig. a).

2 To close the bag, fold the end over a couple of times and force the icing down into the nozzle (Fig. b).

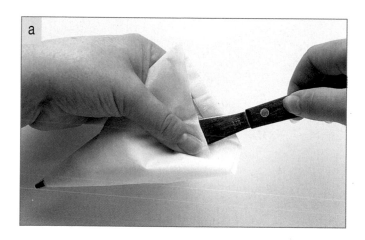

a

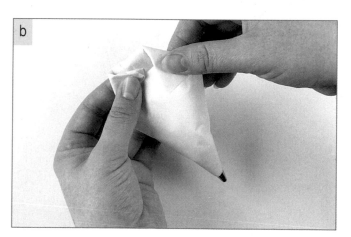

b

Different piping effects

There are many different types of piping nozzle available that enable you to create all sorts of wondrous patterns and effects. Many are made in plastic as well as metal. The difference (apart from the price) being that metal nozzles have slightly more accurate edges and create a sharper effect, and they also tend to last a bit longer.

Piping is just a question of pressure. You squeeze the bag and the icing comes out. Release the pressure and it stops. It really is that simple. That's not to say that you won't have the odd mishap here and there, but most are easy to put right or disguise and after a very short time you'll be amazed at what you can do.

Here are a few of the most common nozzles and the effects you can achieve with them (Fig. a from top to bottom).

NUMBER 2 This has a simple round hole at its tip. It's ideal for piping thin lines, writing, piping dots and tiny "snail trails" around the edges of things. It is also easy to use a nozzle like this to make a simple floral pattern, composed of dots and dashes.

NUMBER 4 This has a bigger hole in the end than the number 2, so can be used for more dramatic effects. You can pipe dots, dashes and even big flowers such as the ones on the Summer flowers cake on page 48.

STAR As its name suggests, the serrated edges of this nozzle are ideal for piping star shapes. You can pipe single stars or even cover a whole cake (see Buttercream flowers on page 42). You can also use a nozzle like this to pipe a line of shells around the edges or base of a cake. See the instructions for "snail trail" opposite.

PETAL Shaped a bit like a teardrop, this nozzle is ideal for piping flowers.

LEAF A very useful nozzle. It enables you to pipe leaf shapes quickly and easily. Wiggle the bag slightly as you pull it away and you end up with a lovely serrated effect.

SNAIL TRAIL (See the first three examples in Fig. a.) This is a common technique used for piping around the base or edges of cakes. Using a nozzle with a plain or star-shaped tip, you squeeze a little icing out of the nozzle, release the pressure and pull along slightly so the icing tapers into a slight point. Keeping the nozzle still in the icing, squeeze another blob out and repeat.

Piping without a nozzle

You can pipe with a bag alone. However, the bag must be used straightaway before the end becomes soggy and distorted or the icing sets and blocks it. Fill and close the bag before cutting anything off the end. (Fig. b from top to bottom.)

SNIP STRAIGHT ACROSS THE END OF THE BAG, REMOVING A TINY TRIANGLE Use this bag as you would a number 2 piping nozzle. The larger the triangle you cut off the end, the thicker the line the bag will produce.

SNIP THE END OF THE BAG INTO A POINT You can make leaf shapes. Squeeze a little icing out of the end and release the pressure. Pull the bag away so that the icing tapers away into a tail.

SNIP A "V" SHAPE INTO THE END OF THE BAG This produces piping that has an interesting ridge along its back.

a

b

Multicoloured piping

On page 28 there is a demonstration, using buttercream, of how you can place more than one colour in a piping bag at a time. It is possible to do this with royal icing too.

Piped flowers

Piping a simple five-petal blossom is a worthwhile technique to try to master as it means that as well as blossoms, you can also pipe violets and primroses. To make violets, colour the icing purple and for primroses, colour it yellow (see page 91).

You will need an icing nail (which looks like a big woodwork nail) or mini turntable which you can revolve in your fingers. Alternatively, you could use a piece of cork stuck on the end of a long nail instead.

1 Place the petal nozzle into a piping bag with about two tablespoons of coloured icing. Fold the end of the bag over to close it.

2 Stick a square of waxed paper onto the top of the piping nail with a dab of icing.

3 With the thick end of the piping nozzle in the centre of the flower, squeeze the bag and turn the nail. Slightly lift the thin edge of the nozzle as you turn, to form a petal. Release the pressure and pull away.

4 Wipe the end of the nozzle. Tuck the nozzle just underneath the edge of the first petal and pipe a second. Repeat, making five petals in total (Fig. c). Remove from the nail or turntable and leave to dry on the paper. Add a yellow dot in the centre to finish (Fig. d, top).

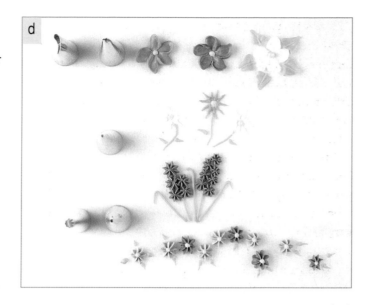

DAISY Pipe white lines fanning out in a circle and pipe a dot of yellow in the centre (Fig. d, centre).

HYACINTH Pipe a central green stem then, using a star nozzle, pipe a few stars either side (Fig. d, bottom).

Piping lettering

There are various ways to position and pipe your message on top of a cake. This technique does require practise, as you have to get used to writing with icing instead of a pen. You will develop your own style of "piping writing" and know instinctively how much space you will need for your message.

SCRIBING A relatively simple way to transfer your message onto a cake covered in sugarpaste or royal icing is by scribing. The cake should have been left to stand overnight so the surface has hardened.

Write your message on a piece of greaseproof paper and place it into position on the cake. Using a scribing tool (a bit like a paintbrush handle with a sharp point on the end) or a dressmaker's pin, trace over the lettering. When you remove the greaseproof paper, you should be able to see your message faintly scratched on the cake's surface. Use this as a guide to pipe over.

FREEHAND This is what you are ultimately aiming for: to be able to write freehand on your cakes. However, even professionals can be caught out sometimes. Beware the word "Congratulations". It's quite long and always seems to take up more room than you think!

Using a letterpress

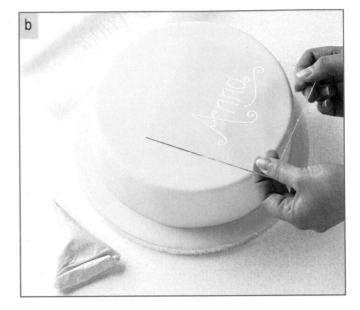

Usually used on sugarpaste or buttercream cakes where they can leave a mark, these ingenious gadgets allow you to build your message on a plaque which you then press into the icing. An imprint is left behind for you to pipe over. There are various makes available which can be bought from cake decorating shops, alternatively you can make your own.

1 Write your message in pencil on a piece of greaseproof paper. Turn the paper over so the message is backwards and place a small piece of perspex on top. Place a number 2 piping nozzle in a piping bag and pipe over the words with royal icing (Fig. a). Leave the lettering to dry.

2 Cover the cake with sugarpaste or buttercream. Turn the perspex over and press into the cake to leave an imprint behind (Fig. b). Use this as a guide to pipe over.

Piped decorations

There are many types of piped royal icing decorations that you can make. Small models, such as the cradle on page 108, are made in sections then stuck together with royal icing. You can pipe onto sugarpaste plaques too. One of their main advantages is that they can be made well in advance. Store the finished decorations in a box away from dust and daylight.

Runouts

This technique of piping an outline then flooding it with watered down royal icing is explained in full in the Baby's cradle and Snowflakes cakes on pages 108 and 112.

However, as well as making shapes, runouts can also be used to make lettering (Fig. c). When dry, gently ease the letters off the waxed paper with a palette knife and fix in place with a dab of royal icing.

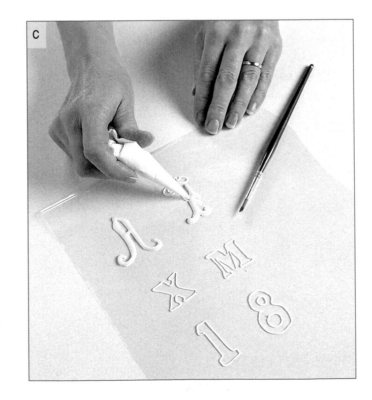

Templates

Baby's cradle (pages 108–109)

Back – make one

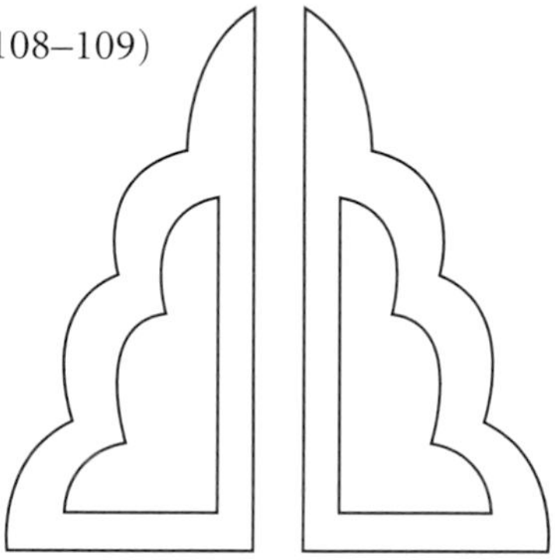

Rockers – make four

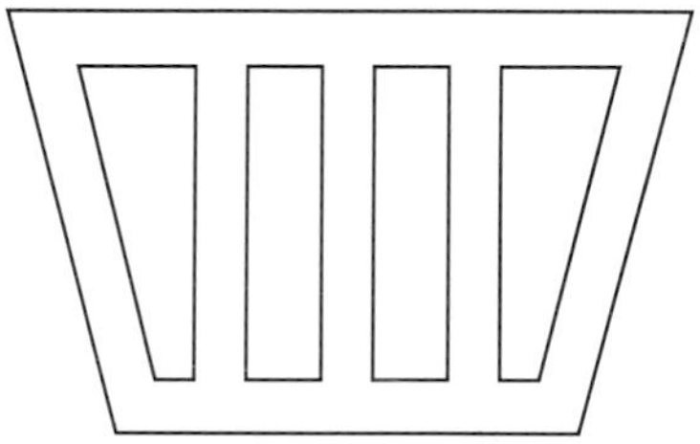

Canopy – make one of each

End of cot – make one

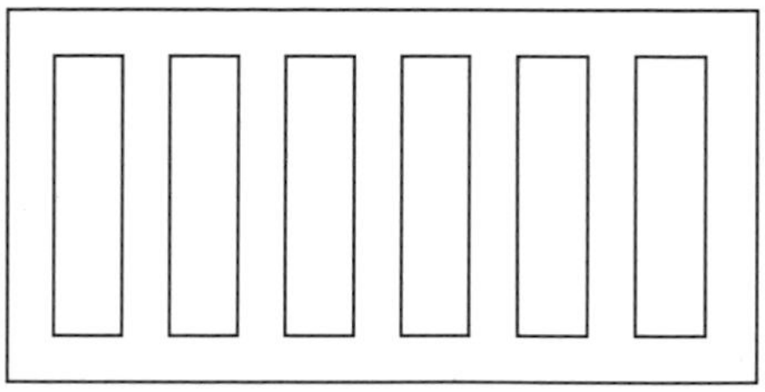

Sides – make two

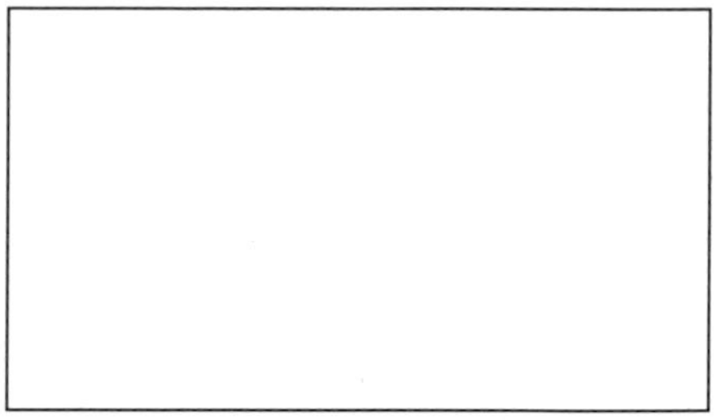

Base – make one

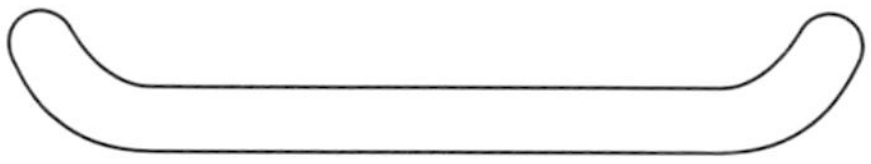

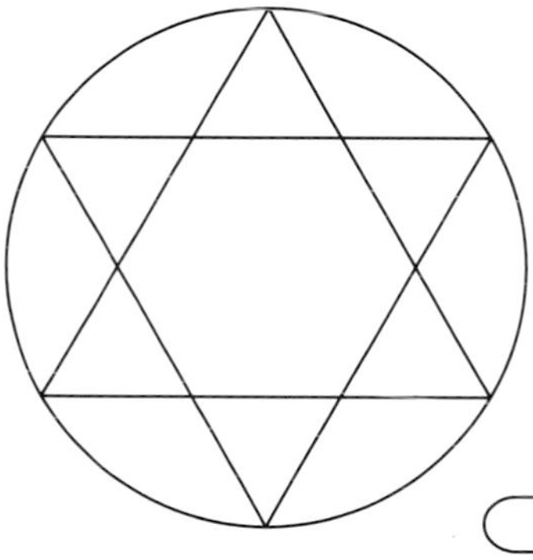

Wedding star (pages 104–105)

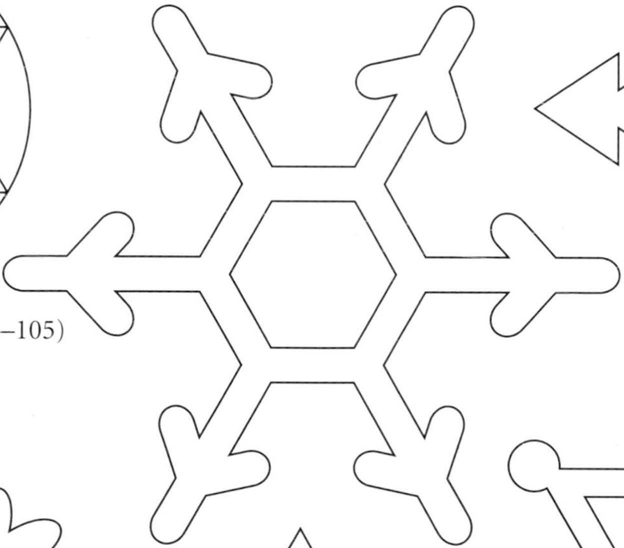

Snowflakes (pages 112–113)

All of the templates are shown at 100%.

Christmas bows ❶

This simple idea makes a stunning Christmas centrepiece. It also works well with coloured ribbon.

ingredients

18-cm (7-in) round fruit cake (see page 14)
3 tbsp brandy (optional)
3 tbsp boiled apricot jam
Icing sugar for rolling out
600g (1¼lb) marzipan
1 quantity white royal icing (see page 90)

equipment

Carving knife
Cocktail stick
23-cm (9-in) round cake board
Pastry brush
Rolling pin
Cake smoother (optional)
Spatula
Small, sharp knife
Palette knife
1m (36in) silver and gold ribbon
Scissors

techniques

Covering a round cake with marzipan
    page 86
Covering a cake with swirled royal icing
    page 91

1 Level the top of the cake and turn it upside-down. Pierce the top a few times with a cocktail stick and drizzle brandy over the top.

2 Place onto the cake board and brush the top and sides with boiled apricot jam.

3 Dust your work surface with icing sugar and knead and roll out the marzipan. Lift the marzipan and place over the top of the cake. Smooth the top and sides, and trim and neaten the base.

4 Spread the royal icing over the cake and board. Swirl it into peaks using the palette knife (Fig. a). Leave the cake to dry.

5 When the icing has hardened, make four bows and stick on to the cake with dabs of royal icing.

variation

You can use any colour scheme on this cake. Here, green and red give the cake a more vibrant and traditional look.

a

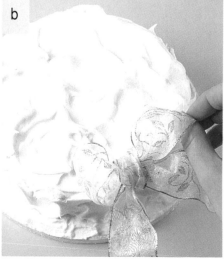

b

tip

As this is a fruit cake, you can make and decorate the cake at the beginning of December to avoid a panic nearer to Christmas.

Wedding star ②

Stylish, elegant, modern – but best of all, easy to do. These instructions are based on using fruit cake and royal icing. However you could use sponge cake as a base if you prefer. Omit the marzipan and split, fill and cover the sponges with scrumptious white chocolate ganache or buttercream instead of royal icing.

ingredients

500g (1lb 2oz) white sugarpaste
Icing sugar, for rolling out
25-cm (10-in) round fruit cake
20-cm (8-in) round fruit cake (alternatively, to save a bit of time, you could hire star-shaped baking tins)
5–6 tbsp brandy (optional)
4–5 tbsp boiled apricot jam
2.6kg (4½lb) marzipan
2 quantities white royal icing (see page 90)

equipment

32-cm (13-in) petal-shaped cake board or a 30-cm (12-in) round board
28-cm (11-in) petal-shaped cake board or a 25-cm (10-in) round board
Rolling pin
Cake smoother (optional)
Small sharp knife
Pencil
Greaseproof or tracing paper
Ruler
Scissors
Carving knife
Pastry brush
Palette knife
1 small church candle
Small square of aluminium foil
About 16 cream rose blooms, washed, dried and stems cut off
About 20 rose leaves, washed and dried
3m (9ft) x 1cm (½in) white ribbon for edging boards (see page 24)
Double-sided tape
2-tier chrome cake stand (see page 24)

1 Cover the cake boards using the all-in-one method (see page 62). Use 250g (8oz) white sugarpaste for the larger board and 150g (5oz) white sugarpaste for the smaller one. Place to one side.

2 Make templates for the cakes. Trace round the tins used for baking the cakes. Draw two identical triangles inside each circle to create a star shape (see diagram on page 101). Cut out.

3 Place the relevant template on top of each cake and cut out (Fig. a).

4 Drizzle each cake with a little brandy if you wish and coat the top with boiled apricot jam.

5 Dust your work surface with icing sugar and roll out 500g (1lb 2oz) marzipan. Run a knife underneath to check it's not stuck to the worktop and lay the largest cake upside down on the marzipan. Cut the marzipan around the cake then turn the cake the right way up.

6 Spread boiled apricot jam around the sides. Roll out 1kg (2lb 4oz) marzipan and cut out a strip about 96cm (38in) long and the same width as the height of the cake, including the marzipan topping.

7 Roll the strip into a loose bandage and unroll around the sides of the cake (Fig b). Because the icing will have a textured finish it is not essential that all the sides are absolutely perfect, however it is important to make sure the cake is sealed in by the marzipan and there are no holes anywhere.

8 Repeat the procedure on the smaller cake using about 350g (12oz) marzipan for the top and 750g (1½lb) marzipan for the sides.

9 Carefully place the cakes into position on the covered boards (see tip opposite). If the cake is well sealed, it can be left in this state in a cake box for up to two weeks, before icing.

10 When ready, cover the cakes with royal icing. Use a palette knife to apply the icing, swirling it into peaks as you go (see Fig. a page 103). Leave a flattish area in the centre of the smaller cake ready for the candle.

11 Stick some double-sided tape around the edge of the boards and then secure the ribbon in place. The ends of the ribbon should meet at the back of the cake.

a

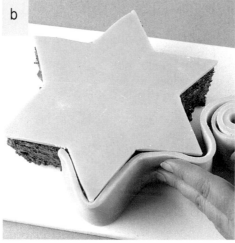

b

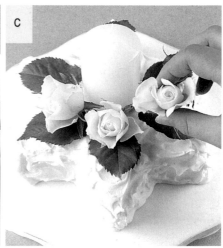

c

12 Add the finishing touches to the cake on the day of the wedding. Place a candle on a small piece of aluminium foil in the centre of the top cake. Lay one large rose leaf over a star point and place a rose on top. Continue around the candle and add a few extra leaves if you wish (Fig. c). Repeat on the lower cake and place the cakes on to the stand.

tips

It is not advisable to use silk flowers with candles because of the possible risk of fire.

It is not essential and will not affect the taste of the cake, but if you want to prevent the sugarpaste beneath the cake from going soggy, place the relevant star template on top of the covered board and cut around it. Remove the icing from the centre of the board. When ready, sit the marzipanned cake in the hole.

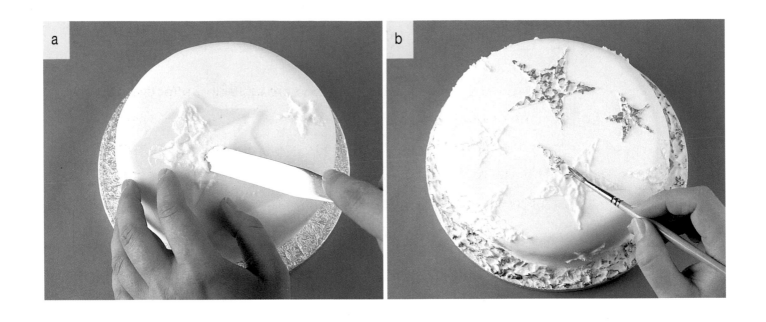

Christmas stars ②

These stencilled stars are very easy to do and are incredibly effective. Depending on your chosen colour scheme, you can leave them white or pick them out with silver or pale blue food colour instead of gold. Instead of using traditional fruit cake covered with royal icing as a base, you could cover a marzipanned fruit cake or buttercreamed sponge cake with sugarpaste instead.

ingredients

(See "Covering the cake" for the amount of icing required to cover cake)

18-cm (7-in) round fruit or sponge cake (see pages 10–14)

1 quantity white royal icing (for making stars; see page 90)

3 tbsp brandy (optional)

3 tbsp boiled apricot jam

Icing sugar, for rolling out

650g (1lb 5oz) marzipan

Edible gold food colour

Edible gold and/or silver balls

equipment

Pencil

Waxed paper, greaseproof paper or baking parchment

Scalpel

Ruler

23-cm (9-in) round cake board

Palette knife

Paintbrush

techniques

Filling and covering a cake with buttercream page 27

Covering a cake with marzipan pages 85–86/sugarpaste 61/royal icing page 94

COVERING THE CAKE

Fruit cake with marzipan and royal icing: follow the instructions on pages 86 and 94. Use about 650g (1lb 5oz) marzipan and two quantities royal icing.

Fruit cake with marzipan and sugarpaste: follow the instructions on pages 85 and 61. Use about 650g (1lb 2oz) marzipan and 500g (1lb 2oz) white sugarpaste. Moisten the marzipan with water before covering it with the sugarpaste.

Sponge cake with sugarpaste: split and fill the cake with buttercream then spread buttercream around the outside (see page 27). Follow the instructions on page 61 for covering with sugarpaste. Use about 500g (1lb 2oz) white sugarpaste.

1 Trace the star shapes onto the paper and cut them out using the scalpel and ruler. Make at least eight as you may only be able to use them once.

2 If not already in place, put the covered cake on the cakeboard. Place the stencil on the cake and stipple some royal icing onto the cake's surface using the flat edge of a palette knife (Fig. a).

3 Lift the stencil off the cake's surface and repeat the process over the sides and top.

4 When you have finished the stars, spread a covering of royal icing over the exposed cake board. Use the flat side of the knife to pat the icing to form little peaks. Leave the cake to dry.

5 When the royal icing has set, pick out the stencil with the gold food colour. Hold the brush almost flat and stroke it across the stars so that the colour only coats the tips of the icing peaks (Fig. b). Do the same on the cakeboard.

6 Stick edible gold balls over the cake to fill the spaces between the stars.

tips

You may be able to find washable, reusable, plastic star-shaped stencils at a cake decorating store which will save you making your own.

You may find it helpful to use tweezers to handle the gold balls as they are tiny.

Baby's cradle ③

This pretty little cradle is made using a technique called royal icing "runouts". The outline of each crib section is piped with royal icing then flooded with slightly watered down icing. It may take a little bit of practice to get this technique right, but the results are worthwhile. One advantage to runouts is that they can be made up to a month in advance. Prepare and ice the cake in exactly the same way as the Christening cake on page 82. Use blue or pink as appropriate.

ingredients
(for the cradle only)
1 quantity white royal icing (see page 90)
15g (½oz) white sugarpaste
5g (⅛oz) flesh-coloured sugarpaste
Food colour for baby's hair
15g (½oz) blue sugarpaste

equipment
(for the cradle only)
Pencil
Greaseproof or tracing paper
Waxed paper or baking parchment
Board or tray
Adhesive tape
Small cups or bowls
Palette knife
Piping bags (see page 96)
No. 1 piping nozzle
Scissors
Small, soft paintbrush
Drinking straw
Tiny ribbon bow

techniques
Runouts page 100
Modelling with sugarpaste page 66

tip
Use a soft, damp paintbrush to smooth away any unwanted blobs of icing along the joins of the cradle.

1 Trace the templates of the cradle components (see page 101) onto greaseproof or tracing paper.

2 Place a piece of waxed paper onto something flat, such as a board or tray, and hold it in place with a small piece of tape at each corner. Slide the tracing paper underneath the waxed paper. Leave an end poking out so that you can move it around freely beneath the top paper.

3 Place about a tablespoon of white royal icing into a cup and beat it thoroughly with a knife to expel any air. Stir in a couple of drops of water to help it flow through the tiny piping nozzle more easily.

4 Place the icing into a piping bag fitted with a number 1 piping nozzle. Close the bag and pipe the outlines of the cradle components.

5 Pipe at least two sides, one pointed end, one bottom end, two canopies, four rockers and one base. It would be wise to pipe extras of each shape as the runouts will be fragile.

6 To make the icing for flooding , place two heaped tablespoons of royal icing into a bowl. Add water drop by drop. Mix until the

consistency is such that when you lift the knife out, the tail it leaves disappears on a count of three.

7 Tip or spoon the icing into a piping bag. Close the bag and snip a tiny triangle off the end. Gently squeeze the bag and using a gentle wiggling motion, fill one of the shapes. Use the tip of a soft, damp paintbrush to coax it into any obstinate corners (Fig. a). Leave to dry for at least 24 hours.

8 When dry, peel the backing off the shapes. Turn the canopy sections over and pipe criss-crossing lines on the back (Fig. b). Stick two sets of rockers together and leave these and the canopies to dry.

9 To make the pillow, make a tiny, white sugarpaste rectangle. Using the tip of a paintbrush handle, press a line of indents down each shorter side to look like a frill (Fig. c).

10 Make a flesh-coloured ball for the head. Use a paintbrush handle to gently push a small dent into the side of the head to resemble a forehead. Make a tiny "U" impression, using the end of a drinking straw, to look like a closed eye.

11 Stick head on the pillow and place both on the cradle base. Add a small sugarpaste oval for the body. Add a tiny flesh ball for his ear and press a small hollow into it with the brush handle. Paint hair with food colour.

12 Carefully stick the sides and the two ends of the cradle around the base using royal icing.

13 Make a tiny white sugarpaste rectangle for the sheet and a larger blue one for the blanket.

14 Using the back of the knife, press a criss-cross pattern into the blanket and lay it onto the edge of the white sheet, leaving about half the white still protruding. Fold the white back over the blue and lay the blanket over the baby.

15 Stick the canopy sections in place. Stick the rockers onto the base of the crib. (You could place a small ball of sugarpaste underneath the cradle to add support while the rockers are drying).

16 Roll two white sugarpaste balls and stick on the two ends of the crib. Stick a tiny bow on top of the canopy. Leave to dry for 24 hours.

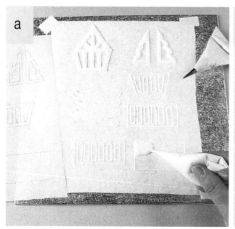

a

b

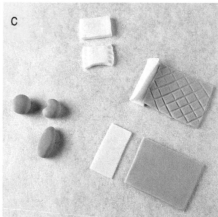

c

Piped flowers ❸

A spiral of pretty piped flowers wind their way around the cake. You could make the flowers up to a month in advance. You can cover the cake with sugarpaste and use sponge instead of fruit cake if you prefer. Instructions are given below.

ingredients

(See "Covering the cake" for the amount of icing required to cover cake)

15-cm (6-in) round fruit or sponge cake (see pages 10 and 14)

1 quantity royal icing (see page 90)

Pink, purple, green, yellow food colour pastes

equipment

20-cm (8-in) round cake board

Scissors

Waxed/silicon paper or baking parchment

No. 57, 58 or 59 petal piping nozzles

Piping bags (see page 96)

Small bowls for mixing colours

Icing nail (or a cork stuck onto a long nail)

No. 2 piping nozzle

Leaf nozzle

Fine paintbrush

techniques

Covering a cake with marzipan pages 85–86/sugarpaste page 61/royal icing page 94

Piping blossom flowers page 99

Piping a snail trail page 98

Piping leaves page 98

COVERING THE CAKE

Fruit cake with marzipan and royal icing: follow the instructions on pages 86 and 94. Use about 600g (1lb 4oz) marzipan and two quantities of royal icing. When the cake has hardened, cover the cake board with royal icing as well (see page 95).

Fruitcake with marzipan and sugarpaste: follow the instructions on pages 85 and 61. Use about 600g (1lb 4oz) marzipan and 500g (1lb 2oz) white sugarpaste. Moisten the marzipan with water before covering it with the sugarpaste. Cover the cake board using the bandage method shown on page 62.

Sponge cake with sugarpaste: split and fill the cake with buttercream then spread buttercream around the outside. Roll out 500g (1lb 2oz) white sugarpaste and cover the cake. Cover the board using the bandage method shown on page 62.

1 Cut out at least 40 waxed paper squares. Place a petal nozzle into a piping bag. Add 2 tablespoons of pink or purple icing. Fold the end of the bag over to close it.

2 Stick a paper square on to the top of the piping nail with a dab of icing. With the thick end of the piping nozzle in the centre of the flower, squeeze the bag and turn the nail. Slightly lift the thin edge of the nozzle as you turn, to form a petal. Release the pressure and pull away.

3 Wipe the end of the nozzle. Tuck the nozzle just underneath the edge of the first petal and pipe a second. Repeat making five petals (Fig. a). It is fiddly and you will need practice.

4 Make about 20 pink and 20 purple flowers and leave them to dry on the wax paper backings for at least 24 hours.

5 When the flowers are ready, place about two tablespoons of white royal icing into a piping bag fitted with the number 2 piping nozzle. Pipe a "snail trail" around the base of the cake. Squeeze a little icing out of the bag, release the pressure and pull slightly to the side, so that the icing tapers and falls on to the cake. Continue like this until you have piped around the whole base.

6 Using a little watered down food colour, paint a spiral guideline around the cake. Start at the base of the cake and work round. Try to keep the width between the lines fairly equal (Fig. b).

7 Peel the backing paper off the flowers and stick the flowers on to the cake with dabs of royal icing.

8 Place about 1 tablespoon of yellow royal icing in a piping bag with a number 2 piping nozzle. Pipe a dot in the centre of each flower.

9 Place a leaf nozzle in a piping bag and add 2 tablespoons of green royal icing. Pipe leaves between the flowers. Squeeze the icing out, release the pressure and pull to create a leaf shape.

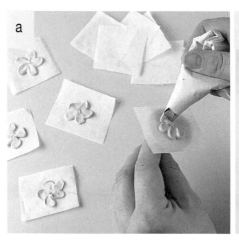

a

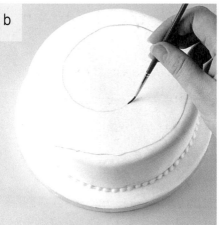

b

tip

You could make the summer flowers on page 46 from royal icing and use these to decorate the cake with instead.

An easier, but still effective alternative to using piped flowers would be to use sugarpaste plunge cutter blossoms (see page 65).

Snowflakes ❸

These snowflakes are made using the royal icing "runout" technique used on the Baby's cradle on page 108. If you don't think you could cope with all the piping you could cut snowflake shapes out of rice paper. If you prefer, you can use sponge instead of fruit cake and cover with sugarpaste instead of royal icing.

ingredients

(See "Covering the cake" for the amount of icing required to cover cake)

20-cm (8-in) round fruit or sponge cake (see pages 10 and 14)

2 quantities white royal icing (for snowflakes; see page 90)

Blue food colour paste

equipment

25-cm (10-in) round cake board

Pencil

Tracing or greaseproof paper

Waxed/silicon paper or baking parchment

Board or tray

Adhesive tape

Small cups/bowls

Palette knife

Piping bags (see page 96)

No. 1 and 2 piping nozzles

Scissors

techniques

Covering a cake with marzipan pages 85–86/ sugarpaste page 61/royal icing page 94

Runouts page 100

Piping a snail trail page 98

COVERING THE CAKE

Fruit cake with marzipan and royal icing: see pages 86 and 94. Use about 750g (1lb 10oz) marzipan and two quantities royal icing. Stir a little blue food colour into the royal icing before coating the cake and board.

Fruit cake with marzipan and sugarpaste: follow the instructions on pages 85 and 61. Use about 750g (1lb 10oz) marzipan and 750g (1lb 10oz) pale blue coloured sugarpaste. Moisten the marzipan with water before covering it with the sugarpaste. Cover the exposed cake board using the leftover sugarpaste and the bandage technique shown on page 62.

Sponge cake with sugarpaste: split and fill the cake with buttercream then spread buttercream around the outside. Roll out and cover the cake with 750g (1lb 10oz) of pale blue coloured sugarpaste. Cover the exposed cake board with the leftover sugarpaste using the bandage technique shown on page 62.

tip

The snowflakes can be made well in advance, so you can prepare them before the Christmas panic sets in.

1 Trace the snowflake templates on page 101 on to tracing paper. Place a piece of waxed paper onto something flat such as a board or tray and hold it in place with a piece of tape at each corner. Slide the tracing paper underneath the waxed paper (see Fig. a page 109).

2 Place about 1 tablespoon of white royal icing into a cup and beat it thoroughly with a knife to expel any air. Stir in a couple of drops of water to help it flow through the tiny piping nozzle more easily. The icing should still hold its shape when piped.

3 Place the icing into a piping bag fitted with a number 1 piping nozzle. Pipe over the outlines of the snowflakes. Pipe at least 16 outlines to allow for breakages (see Fig. a on page 109).

4 Place about 2 tablespoons of royal icing into a bowl. Add a few drops of water and mix in. Continue to add water, drop by drop, and mix it in until the icing has reached such a consistency that when you lift the knife out, the tail it leaves behind disappears on a count of three.

5 Tip or spoon the icing into a piping bag. Close the bag and snip a tiny triangle off the end. Gently squeeze the end and using a gentle wiggling motion, fill one of the shapes (see Fig. a page 109). Use the tip of a soft, damp paintbrush to coax it into any obstinate corners. Leave the shapes to dry for at least 24 hours.

6 Place about 1 tablespoon of royal icing into a piping bag fitted with a number 2 piping nozzle. Pipe a "snail trail" around the base of the cake. Squeeze a bit of icing out, release the pressure and pull slightly to the side so that the icing forms a tail. Repeat all the way round the cake (Fig. a).

7 When the snowflakes are dry, slide a palette knife beneath them to gently ease them off the paper (Fig. b).

8 Place the snowflakes into position and stick with dabs of royal icing.

9 Pipe royal icing dots between the snowflakes to finish off (Fig. c).

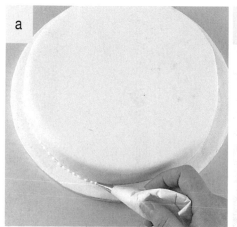

a

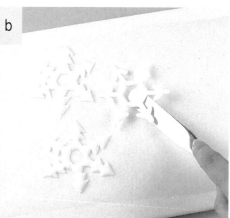

b

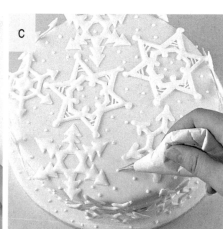

c

CHOCOLATE

As well as being delicious, chocolate is extremely versatile too. It can be used to cover a cake, moulded into decorations and mixed with cream to make ganache. This chapter contains ideas for all sorts of occasions. There's even a simple recipe for truffles that uses up all those bits of leftover cake (see page 118).

Types of chocolate

There are four basic grades of chocolate to choose from and all are available in dark, milk or white forms. I would advise that you use either dessert or baking chocolate as they are easy to handle.

DESSERT OR EATING CHOCOLATE This is the product you'll find in the sweet shop. Dark chocolate has the strongest flavour and tends to be quite hard when you bite into it. Milk chocolate is softer to the bite and sweeter. White is sweeter still and actually doesn't taste of chocolate at all. All of these types can be used in cooking. A purist would argue that you should only use dark chocolate containing a minimum of 70 percent cocoa solids for cooking, but it is your choice.

COUVERTURE Because it is made entirely with cocoa butter couverture is the most expensive type of chocolate and is considered by most experts to be the best chocolate to use in cooking. However, it has to be tempered (heated and cooled to an exact temperature) before use so it's not that easy for a beginner to use.

BAKING/COOKING CHOCOLATE This type of chocolate melts easily and is ideal for the beginner. The taste varies from brand to brand and, in fact, some supermarket own brands are now so good it is very hard to tell them apart from dessert chocolate.

CHOCOLATE FLAVOURED CAKE COVERING This is not actually chocolate at all, it is merely chocolate-flavoured. The taste is weak and it tends to have a soft and greasy texture. It melts and sets very quickly, which can be useful if you are in a hurry. Because it is much cheaper than any other type of chocolate it may be worth using to experiment with, particularly if you have never worked with chocolate before.

Melting chocolate

When melting chocolate you must not get any water, steam or condensation in the chocolate. If you do, it will become thick, gritty and unusable.

1 Break the chocolate into small pieces and place in a heatproof bowl (Fig. a).

2 Place the bowl over a saucepan of water. The water should not touch the base of the bowl. Heat the water and simmer until the chocolate has melted (Fig. b).

Alternative method
Break the chocolate into pieces into a bowl that is microwave-safe. Heat on high for 90 seconds. Stir and repeat. Don't let it overcook otherwise it will burn.

RIGHT *You can make all sorts of decorations using chocolate, all of which are very easy to make. These include chocolate leaves, runouts, squiggles and shapes. See page 117 for instructions.*

Covering a cake with melted chocolate

A simple way to cover a cake is to pour chocolate over it. The cake can be plain or pre-iced with ganache.

1 Place the cake on a rack and pour the chocolate over the top (Fig. a). The cake must be at room temperature.

2 Lightly bang the rack up and down a few times to encourage the chocolate to fully cover the cake and to dislodge any air bubbles (Fig. b). Leave to set.

Chocolate ganache

Ganache is a spread made out of a mixture of cream and melted chocolate. Made using white or dark chocolate, it can be used to fill and cover gateau-type cakes, but would not normally be used with sugarpaste designs.

ingredients
300g (10oz) dark or white chocolate, broken into pieces
600ml (1pt) double cream

1 Place the broken chocolate into a large bowl.

2 Gently heat the cream in a saucepan and bring up to boiling point. Remove from the heat and pour over the chocolate.

3 Leave for 3 minutes then stir until the chocolate has melted.

4 Leave to cool completely then whisk to a light, whipped consistency. Cover and place in the fridge for at least half an hour or until required.

5 When ready to use, remove from the fridge. If it is still a little sloppy, beat until thick.

Piping with ganache
It is also possible to pipe with chocolate ganache. You could pipe a milk chocolate border onto a cake that has been covered in white chocolate, or vice versa (Fig. c). Add some chocolate leaves or a few chocolate-dipped fruits for a stylish yet simple cake for a special occasion.

Chocolate leaves

An effective decoration that is incredibly easy to make.

1 Select some well proportioned rose leaves. Wash and dry them on absorbent kitchen paper.

2 Melt some chocolate (see page 114). Hold a leaf by the stalk and press the underside (this side produces a better vein effect) into the melted chocolate. Leave to dry on waxed or greaseproof paper.

3 When the leaves have set, carefully peel the real leaf off the chocolate one (see Fig. b on page 136).

Dipped fruits

You can use plain, milk or white chocolate and many different kinds of fruit, including strawberries, grapes, cherries and redcurrants.

1 Wash and dry the fruit on absorbent kitchen paper. Melt the chocolate (see page 114).

2 Dip the fruit into the chocolate so that it is half covered. Leave to set on waxed or greaseproof paper (Fig. d).

Chocolate runouts

Another way to make simple shapes is to make runouts. The basic principle is exactly the same as that for making royal icing runouts (see page 100). You can vary the colours too – pipe an outline with dark chocolate and fill it with white, for example.

1 Place some melted chocolate into a piping bag. Fold the end of the bag to close it and snip a triangle off the end.

2 Pipe the outline of a simple shape, such as a heart, onto waxed paper or baking parchment.

3 Place some more melted chocolate in another bag. Snip a bigger triangle off the end and fill in the chocolate outline (Fig. e).

Chocolate shapes

There are a couple of ways of making decorative chocolate shapes and both are very simple.

Solid shapes

Cut the shapes you want out of rice paper. Dip one side of the rice paper shape into melted chocolate. Leave to dry. As it is edible, you can either leave the paper on or peel it off. This technique is used and explained in full in the Chocolate shapes and Chocolate extravaganza cakes on pages 130 and 134.

Squiggles or shape outlines

Simply pipe the shape, using melted chocolate, onto a sheet of waxed or greaseproof paper. Leave to set.

Chocolate modelling paste

There are all sorts of different ways of making chocolate modelling paste, but the easiest way to make it is to knead some cocoa powder into a piece of marzipan. There are no hard and fast rules about amounts; obviously the more you add, the darker the colour will be. Use as normal marzipan (see page 88).

If the marzipan is hard to knead, microwave it for 10–15 seconds to soften it. Repeat if necessary but don't overdo it, otherwise the oils in the marzipan could get very hot and burn.

Quick chocolate rose

This is a very simple way to make a rose using chocolate modelling paste. Of course, it would work using uncoloured marzipan and sugarpaste too (Fig. a).

1 Take about 15g (½oz) of chocolate marzipan. Roll it into a thin sausage shape.

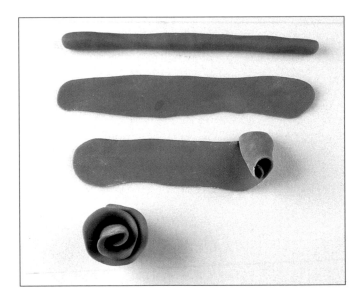

2 Flatten the sausage shape into a thin strip. Press along one long edge to make it thinner. Paint a line of water along the other long edge.

3 Carefully roll the marzipan up like a bandage, the thinnest edge should form the flower.

4 Tweak the edges slightly to improve the rose shape.

Chocolate truffles

This is a great way to use up those left over pieces of cake. This recipe works equally well using sponge, chocolate or fruit cake and with any type of chocolate.

1 Break up the cake into crumbs and place in a bowl.

2 Melt some chocolate. You will need approximately 30g (1oz) of chocolate for every 30g (1oz) of cake crumb.

3 Stir the chocolate into the crumbs (Fig. b).

4 Roll the mixture into balls. Place in petit fours cases if you wish.

5 Decorate with melted chocolate and sweets.

Templates

All of the templates are shown at 100%.

Cocoa painting
(pages 126–127)
Make five.

Patterns for plaques.

Chocolate shapes (pages 130–131)
Make nine of each shape.

Quick chocolate cake ❶

This cake has been decorated using techniques that granny would have used. It's a traditional cake that's perfect for afternoon tea – it looks just perfect, yet is so simple.

ingredients

2 × 18-cm (7-in) chocolate cakes baked in
    sandwich tins or 1 cake baked in a
    normal cake tin, cut in half (see
    page 12)
1 quantity vanilla buttercream (see
    page 26)
1 tsp cocoa powder
Decoration for top of cake (shop-bought
    lattice shapes/leaves/sweets etc.)

equipment

Carving knife
Palette knife
20-cm (8-in) round cake board or plate
Paper doily
Small sieve or tea strainer

techniques

Baking a cake page 12
Making buttercream page 26
Filling and covering a cake with
    buttercream page 27

1 Split the cake horizontally in half. Sandwich the two cake layers together with a liberal spreading of buttercream. Place cake on board. Spread buttercream smoothly over the top of the cake.

2 Lay the paper doily on top of the cake. Place the cocoa powder in the sieve and gently tap it, moving it over the doily (Fig. a).

3 Carefully peel back the doily to reveal a pattern underneath (Fig. b).

4 Place a dab of buttercream and a few chocolate decorations in the centre of the cake to finish off.

tips

Chocolate leaves are easy to make if you want to keep the whole design homemade. See page 117 to find out how to make them.

You can freeze the buttercreamed cake if you wish. Allow it to defrost thoroughly and make sure that all of the condensation has evaporated before decorating it with the cocoa.

Instead of cocoa you could decorate the cake with sweets or chocolate buttons instead.

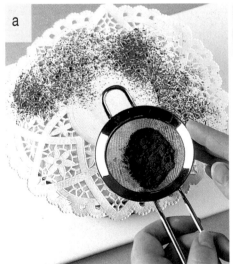

a

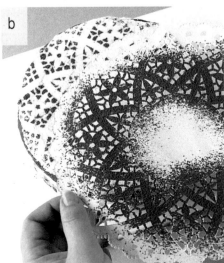

b

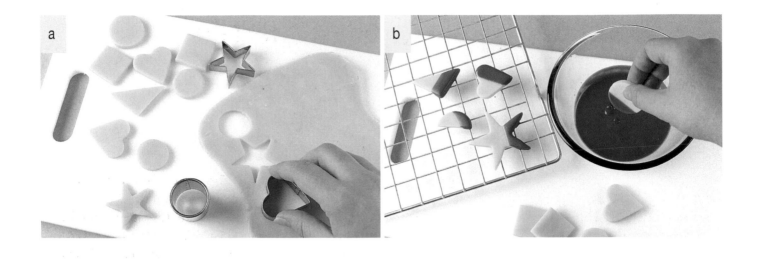

Marzipan chocolates ❶

This is a very easy cake to put together. The difficult part is stopping yourself from nibbling and sampling as you go!

ingredients

Icing sugar, for rolling out

250g (8oz) golden marzipan

150g (5oz) milk chocolate

15-cm (6-in) round sponge cake (see page 10

2 quantities chocolate buttercream (see page 26) or 1 quantity chocolate ganache (see page 116)

equipment

Rolling pin

Assorted cutters

Heatproof bowl

Small saucepan

Cooling rack

Carving knife

Palette knife

20-cm (8-in) round cake board

techniques

Melting chocolate page 114

Filling and covering a cake with buttercream or ganache page 27 or 116

variation

Put a few marzipan chocolates into a box and create a lovely little present for someone.

1 Prepare the chocolates. Dust your work surface with icing sugar and knead and roll out the marzipan to a thickness of about 5mm (¼in). Using the cutters, cut out about 40 shapes (Fig. a).

2 Melt the milk chocolate in a heatproof bowl. Dip each shape into the chocolate and place on a cooling rack to harden (Fig. b).

3 When the chocolates are set, prepare the cake. Slice the cake into two or three layers and then sandwich back together with buttercream or ganache. Place the cake on a board.

4 Spread and swirl the icing over the outside of the cake. Press the marzipan shapes into the chocolate covering.

Easter cake ❶

Here's a cake that's simple to put together and will brighten up any
Easter tea-table.

chocolate

a

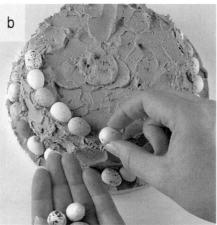

b

ingredients

50g (1¾oz) milk chocolate

50g (1¾oz) cereal

15-cm (6-in) round sponge cake (see
    page 10)

1 quantity chocolate buttercream (see
    page 26)

Mini chocolate eggs

equipment

Heatproof bowl

Small saucepan

Small bowl to use as mould for nest

Carving knife

Palette knife

20-cm (8-in) round cake board

About 6 chick cake decorations

techniques

Melting chocolate page 114

Filling and covering a cake with
    buttercream page 27

1 To make the nest, melt the
chocolate and break up the cereal.
Mix the two together and spoon
the mixture into a small bowl
(Fig. a). Leave to set.

2 To prepare the cake, level the top
and turn the cake upside down.
Split it into two or three layers and
re-assemble, filling the layers with
buttercream.

3 Place the cake onto the cake board
and cover the top, sides and
exposed cake board with
buttercream.

4 Press a line of chocolate eggs
around the top and bottom of the
cake (Fig. b).

5 When the nest has set, place it on
top of the cake and fill with little
chicks. You could add a few extra
eggs as well if you wish.

tip

Instead of using shop-bought
chocolate eggs, you could make
your own eggs out of sugarpaste or
use sugared almonds.

variation

This cake was decorated with an
Easter teddy whose body is a
chocolate egg.

Roll 30g (1oz) golden marzipan into a
sausage for his legs. Place the egg
in the centre and bend the marzipan
round it to hold the egg steady.
Tweak the ends into feet.

Make a 15g (½oz) marzipan ball for
his head and stick on top of the
egg. Add a marzipan oval for his
muzzle and two tiny balls for his
ears. Press the end of a paintbrush
into each ear and into the lower part
of his muzzle to make a mouth. Add
three black food colour dots for his
eyes and nose.

Make two 5g (⅛oz) sausage shapes
for his arms and stick onto the body.

Warning! To avoid arguments it might
be wise to make enough spare teddies
so that everyone can have one!

Cocoa painting ❷

Cocoa painting is a traditional technique that's often overlooked nowadays. Of course, you don't have to paint a pattern on your cake, you could paint an actual picture, perhaps of a much-loved pet or place. The cocoa gives the image a sepia look, like that of an old photograph.

ingredients

300g (10oz) white sugarpaste
Icing sugar, for rolling out
1 tsp white fat
1 tsp cocoa powder
15-cm (6-in) square sponge cake (see page 10)
2 quantities chocolate buttercream (see page 26)

equipment

Rolling pin
Cutter or template (see page 119) for plaques
Saucer
Small saucepan
Fine paintbrush
Scalpel
Carving knife
Palette knife
20-cm (8-in) square cake board
Star piping nozzle (optional; see tip opposite)
Piping bag (see page 96)

techniques

Making a plaque page 66
Filling and covering a cake with buttercream page 27
Piping with buttercream page 98

1 To make the plaques, roll out the sugarpaste and cut out a thin oval, either with a cutter or using the template on page 119. Cut out four more, re-kneading and re-rolling the sugarpaste as necessary. If you have time, leave them to harden for 12 hours, turning over after 5-6 hours.

2 To paint the plaques, melt a little white fat on a saucer over a pan of hot water. Remove the pan from the heat but leave the saucer in place while you work to keep the fat melted.

3 Mix a little cocoa powder and melted fat together with the paintbrush (Fig. a).

4 Lightly paint the outline of the picture on to a plaque and fill it in (Fig. b). If you do not want to paint the pattern freehand, trace the patterns on page 119 and scribe them onto the plaque (see page 99). Remember that you can always add more but you can't take it off, so build the picture up gradually.

5 If you want to create highlights or thin, line effects, you can scratch bits off with the tip of a clean, sharp scalpel (Fig. c).

6 Level the top of the cake and turn it upside-down. Slice into two or three layers and re-assemble it, filling the layers with buttercream.

7 Place the cake onto the cake board and spread buttercream over the top and sides. Spread buttercream over the exposed areas of the cake board as well.

8 Place the plaques into position. Press them gently into the buttercream to hold them in place.

9 Place a star piping nozzle into a piping bag and spoon 2–3 tablespoons of buttercream into the bag. Pipe around the outsides of the plaques and the edges and base of the cake. Vary the shades of brown if you wish by adding more cocoa to the buttercream.

tips

If you don't want to pipe buttercream onto the cake, stick chocolate buttons or other chocolate sweets around it instead.

Use white candles in white birthday cake candleholders and stand them in the chocolate buttercream on top of the cake. Don't try to poke them through the sugarpaste plaque.

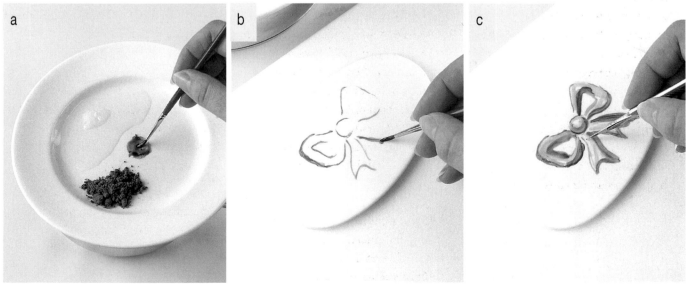

a

b

c

Chocolate feathers ❷

You can make the chocolate feathers a few days in advance if you wish. Just store them somewhere dry where people won't be tempted to pinch them.

ingredients
100g (4oz) milk chocolate
100g (4oz) plain chocolate
100g (4oz) white chocolate
20-cm (8-in) round sponge cake (see
    page 10)
2 quantities white chocolate buttercream
    (see page 26) or 1 quantity white
    chocolate ganache (see page 116)

equipment
Greaseproof paper or baking parchment
Tray
Heatproof bowls for melting chocolate
Small saucepan
About 6 piping bags (see page 96)
Cup
Scissors
Sharp pointed knife
Carving knife
Palette knife
25-cm (10-in) round cake board

techniques
Melting chocolate page 114
Making a piping bag page 97
Filling and covering a cake with
    buttercream page 27

1 Make the feathers first so that they have time to harden. Place a large sheet of greaseproof paper on a tray. Melt the milk chocolate in a bowl either in a microwave or over a pan of simmering water.

2 Place a piping bag into a cup and tip in some of the chocolate. Carefully fold over the ends of the bag to close it and snip a tiny triangle off the end.

3 Pipe a thick line (it can be either straight or wavy) of chocolate onto the greaseproof paper (Fig. a). It's not essential to use a bag, you can drizzle a line with a spoon if you prefer, but a bag makes things much easier and is less sticky.

4 Using the tip of a sharp knife, poke and drag the chocolate from the centre of the line outwards to make a point. Continue down both sides of the line fanning the chocolate outwards (Fig. b). Make about 20 to allow for breakages and chocolate thieves!

5 Repeat procedure with the dark and white chocolate and leave to harden in a cool, dry place.

6 When the feathers are ready, prepare the cake. Level the top and turn it upside down. Slice it into two or three horizontal layers and re-assemble it, sandwiching the layers together with buttercream.

7 Put cake onto cake board. Spread buttercream around the sides and top of the cake.

8 Gently slide a palette knife under a feather and ease it off the backing paper. Place the feather in position on the cake. Make a ring around the base and top of the cake and place a few in the centre.

tips
Make the piped lines of chocolate quite thick. If the feathers are too thin, they'll just snap and be impossible to use. You can also mix colours by piping a line of milk and white chocolate together.

Candles should be placed in holders inside the top ring of feathers but away from the central ones. Use white candles and holders.

a

b

Chocolate shapes ❷

Dipping rice paper into melted chocolate is an easy way to make effective chocolate shapes. Because the rice paper is edible, you can either leave it on the back or peel it off when they've hardened.

ingredients

Rice paper

100g (3½oz) milk chocolate

100g (3½oz) dark chocolate

15-cm (6-in) round sponge cake (see page 10)

2 quantities white chocolate buttercream (see page 26) or 1 quantity white chocolate ganache (see page 116)

equipment

Pencil

Rice paper

Scissors

Waxed paper or baking parchment

Tray

Heatproof bowl

Small saucepan

2 piping bags (see page 96)

20-cm (8-in) round cake board

techniques

Melting chocolate page 114

Filling and covering a cake with buttercream page 27

1 Using rice paper, trace and cut out about nine each of the heart, square, circle, moon and star templates (see page 119). Cut just inside the pencil marks.

2 Place some baking parchment or waxed paper on to a tray.

3 Melt the milk chocolate. Dip a rice paper shape into the chocolate (Fig. a). Coat one side then place onto the tray.

4 Make four or five shapes. Holding both edges of the tray, bang it on your work surface a couple of times to dislodge any air bubbles.

5 Repeat this procedure until half of the rice paper shapes have been used.

6 Tip any leftover melted chocolate into a piping bag. Fold the end to close it and snip a tiny triangle off the end. Pipe a squiggle directly on to the covered tray (Fig. b).

7 Repeat the above procedure with the dark chocolate.

8 When the chocolate shapes have set, prepare the cake. Slice it into three layers and re-assemble, filling the layers with buttercream or ganache.

9 Put the cake onto the cake board. Spread a thick coating of buttercream or ganache around the outside of the cake.

10 Peel the rice paper off the shapes (or leave it on, it's up to you) and press them into the icing.

tips

If you're feeling really ambitious you could pipe the recipient's name in chocolate, either in single letters or in joined-up writing.

Only use a few candles and have them alight for as little time as possible as the heat might melt the chocolate.

a

b

Monster cup cake ❷

This cake is baked in a pudding bowl to give it its authentic shape. The enormous paper cake case is actually a paper cake tin liner which you can buy from kitchen or cake decoration equipment shops.

ingredients

1 chocolate pudding bowl cake (see page 10 and step 1 right)
Icing sugar for rolling out
150g (5oz) white sugarpaste
15g (½oz) red sugarpaste
75g (2¾oz) grey sugarpaste
Water for sticking
Black food colour or black food colour pen

equipment

15-cm (6-in) round cake tin liner
Rolling pin
Sharp knife
Paintbrush
About an 18-cm (7-in) round plate or cake board
15-cm (6-in) round paper cake tin liner

techniques

Baking a pudding bowl cake page 10
Working with sugarpaste page 60

1 Mix up a three-egg sponge mixture (see page 10). Add 1 tablespoon of cocoa. Place the liner in the bowl, turn the mixture into it and bake.

2 When the cake is cool, roll out the white sugarpaste. Holding a sharp knife virtually upright, cut out a wiggly, vaguely circular shape for the white topping (Fig. a). Keep the excess.

3 Place the topping on to the cake. Roll about 10g (⅓oz) red sugarpaste into a ball for the cherry and stick on top of the cake with a dab of water.

4 To make the mouse, roll about 50g (1½oz) grey sugarpaste into a conical shape for the mouse's body. Bend the pointed end over to form the head (Fig. b). Using the end of a paintbrush, poke an oval hole for his outraged mouth.

5 Make two 5g (⅙oz) oval shapes for the feet and stick either side of his body. Make a couple of tiny lines in the end of each foot with the tip of the knife.

6 Make two tiny white balls for the eyes and stick on to the head with little dabs of water. Add tiny black dots for the pupils using black food colour and a fine brush or a black food colour pen.

7 Knead a tiny bit of red sugarpaste into a little bit of white to make a pink colour. Make a tiny ball for the nose and a wiggly string for the tail. Stick both in position and press a few lines down the length of the tail.

8 Make two tiny grey strings for arms. Bend into "S" shapes and stick on the side of the body. Make two tiny grey ball shapes for the ears and stick on the side of the head. Poke the end of a paintbrush into each ear to both add definition and to push it securely on to the head.

9 Place the cake and the mouse in position on the plate or cake board. Use a dab of water to hold the mouse in place if necessary.

tip

To make a chocolate chip cake, stir a handful of chocolate chips into the cake mixture before baking.

a

b

Chocolate extravaganza ❷

Deceptively easy and devilishly tasty. There really is no better cake to make for the favourite chocoholic in your life! If you're prepared for a little bit more work, you could fill the top of the cake with homemade truffles (see page 118). Both versions of this cake would be ideal for Mothering Sunday.

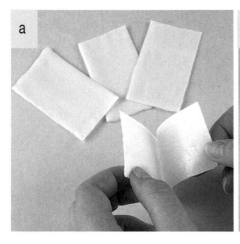

a

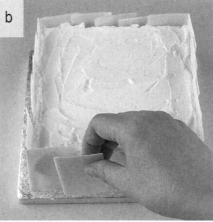

b

ingredients

1 pack rice paper

150g (5oz) white chocolate

15-cm (6-in) square sponge cake (see
    page 10)

1 quantity white chocolate buttercream
    (see page 26) or ganache (see
    page 116)

Assorted chocolates

equipment

Scissors

Waxed paper or baking parchment

Tray

Heatproof bowl

Small saucepan

Carving knife

Palette knife

20-cm (8-in) square cake board

1m (36in) ribbon

techniques

Melting chocolate page 114

Making chocolate shapes page 117

Filling and covering a cake with
    buttercream page 27

1 Cut the rice paper into 24
rectangles about 4 × 8cm (1½ ×
3in). They must stand higher than
the edge of the cake. Place some
baking parchment on to a tray.

2 Melt the chocolate. Dip the
smooth side of a rectangle shape
into the chocolate (see Fig. a page
131). Place onto the tray.

3 Coat four or five rectangles then,
holding both edges of the tray,
bang it on your work surface a
couple of times to dislodge any air
bubbles. Repeat this procedure
until all the rectangles have been
covered. Leave to set.

4 To prepare the cake, level the top
and turn it upside down. Slice into
two or three layers and re-assemble,
filling the layers with buttercream
or ganache.

5 Spread icing over the sides and top
of the cake.

6 Peel the rice paper backing off the
strips (Fig. a). It is edible, so you
can leave it on if you find it too
fiddly to peel off.

7 Press the white chocolate strips
around the sides of the cake,
overlapping them as you go
(Fig. b). Use six per side.

8 Fill the top with chocolates and
gently tie a bow around the
outside of the cake.

variation

Fill the top of the cake with rose
blooms for an elegant, luxurious treat.
Wash the flowers and leaves well with
cold water and dry thoroughly on
kitchen towel before using.

a

b

chocolate

White chocolate ring ❷

Chocolate leaves are extremely simple to make and give the traditional, humble chocolate cake a lavish new look! You could use a mixture of dark, milk and white chocolate leaves if you wish.

ingredients

100g (3½oz) white chocolate

18-cm (7-in) round sponge cake (see page 10)

1 quantity chocolate buttercream (see page 26) or ganache (see page 116)

equipment

About 25 rose leaves

Kitchen paper

Waxed paper or baking parchment

Tray

Heatproof bowl

Carving knife

23-cm (9-in) round plate or cake board

Palette knife

techniques

Melting chocolate page 114

Filling and covering a cake with buttercream page 27

1 Wash the rose leaves and dry them on absorbent kitchen paper. Place some waxed paper or baking parchment on a tray. Melt the chocolate.

2 Holding a rose leaf by its stalk, dip the underside of the leaf into the chocolate (Fig. a). Lay on the waxed paper to dry.

3 To prepare the cake, slice it horizontally and fill with chocolate buttercream or ganache.

4 Place the cake onto a plate or cake board and spread a thick covering of buttercream or ganache over the top and sides.

5 When set, peel the rose leaves away from the chocolate (Fig b).

6 Gently press the leaves in a ring formation around the cake.

tip

If you want to add a bit of colour, lay a few rosebuds around the edge of the plate.

variation

Construct this cake in exactly the same way, except place leaves over the top as well. Sprinkle the whole cake with a little sieved cocoa powder. You could make milk and plain chocolate leaves as well if you wish.

Choc 'n' nut ❷

Beware of this cake! It may be small, but it is incredibly rich and gorgeous. The use of shop-bought hazelnut spread as a cake covering saves time. However, if you don't like nuts, you can use chocolate buttercream or ganache, smothered with vermicelli instead.

ingredients
15-cm (6-in) round sponge cake (see page 10)
2 large jars hazelnut chocolate spread
100g (3½oz) chopped nuts
90g (3oz) golden marzipan
Cocoa powder
Black food colour or black food colour pen
1 nut (pecan, hazelnut etc.)

equipment
Carving knife
Palette knife
20-cm (8-in) round cake board
Small, sharp knife
Fine paintbrush

techniques
Filling and covering a cake with buttercream page 27
Modelling with marzipan page 88

1 Level the top of the cake and slice the cake horizontally into two or three layers. Re-assemble the cake, sandwiching it together with hazelnut spread. Place the cake onto the cake board.

2 Coat the top and sides of the cake liberally with hazelnut spread. Cover the exposed cake board too.

3 Carefully press handfuls of chopped nuts into the sides of the cake (Fig. a). You will get messy!

4 Put about 15g (½oz) of the marzipan aside for making the tail. Knead about 1 teaspoon of cocoa powder into the rest to turn it a dark brown colour.

5 Make a 30g (1oz) conical shape for the squirrel's body. Bend the pointed end forwards slightly to make the head. Press a line into the head with a knife to make a mouth (Fig. b).

6 Make a 10g (⅓oz) chunky sausage shape for a leg. Squash one end to make the thigh and stick against the squirrel's body with a dab of water. Repeat on the other side with the second leg.

7 Make two tiny sausage shapes for arms. Stick onto the squirrel's body. Position a nut in front of his tummy and place his arms onto the nut so that it looks as though the squirrel's holding it.

8 Make two triangles for the ears and stick onto the head. Add two black food colour dots for eyes.

9 Roll the leftover golden marzipan into a flattish oval. Bend into an "S" shape and stick onto the back. Press a few lines into the tail with the back of a knife.

10 Place the squirrel onto the centre of the cake and sprinkle a few nuts around it.

tip
Before covering the sides of the cake with the nuts, fold a sheet of greaseproof paper in half. Open the paper up and stand the cake on top. When finished, remove the cake, lift the paper up, fold it in half and pour the excess nuts back into the packet.

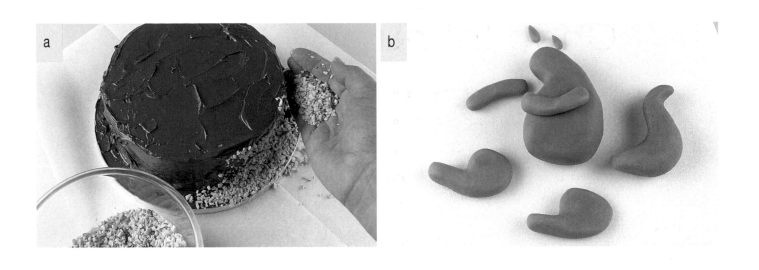

SUPPLIERS

UK

Blue Ribbons Sugarcraft Centre
110 Walton Road
Easy Molesey
Surrey KT8 0HP
Tel: (020) 8941 1591
Email: blueribbons.co.uk
www.blueribbons.co.uk
Supply wide range of equipment, decorations and ingredients.

The British Sugarcraft Guild
Wellington House
Messeter Place
London SE9 5DP
Tel: (020) 8859 6943

The Cake Makers Depot
57 The Tything
Worcester WR1 1JT
Tel: (01905) 25468

Cake Pix
www.cakepix.co.uk
Print photos, clip art and other attractive designs on to special sheets of icing to add to the top of a celebration cake.

Confectionery Supplies
29–31 Lower Cathedral Road
Cardiff CF1 8LU
Tel: (01222) 372161
Also outlets in Bristol, Hereford and Swansea.

Cookcraft
Welcome House
High Street
Cheslyn Hay
Walsall
West Midlands
Tel: (01922) 416555
Fax: (01922) 418844
Email: info@cookcraft.com
www.cookcraft.com
Wide range of cookware and bakeware. Visit store or shop on-line.

Culpitt Ltd
Jubilee Industrial Estate
Ashington NE63 8UQ
Tel: (01670) 814545
Freephone enquiry line: 0845 601 0574
www.culpitt.com
Distributor of cake decorations, telephone for your nearest retail outlet.

Divertimenti
139/141 Fulham Road
London SW3 6SD
Tel: (020) 7581 8065
Fax: (020) 7823 9429
Email: Fulhamroad@divertimenti.co.uk
or
33/34 Marylebone High Street
London W1U 4PT
Tel: (020) 7935 0689
Fax: (020) 7224 0058
Email: sales@divertimenti.co.uk
www.divertimenti.co.uk
Stock a wide range of bakeware. Visit one of the stores or shop on-line.

Halstead Icing
The Old Surgery
Weavers Court
Halstead
Essex CO9 2JN
Tel/Fax: (01787) 472924
www.halsteadicing.co.uk
Sell large range of sugarcraft equipment, ribbons, boards and cutters. Offer cake tin, stand and knife hire service. No mail order.

The Icing on the Cake
15 Allhallows Lane
Kendal
Cumbria LA9 4JH
Tel: (01539) 735591
Email: sales@the-icing-on-the-cake.co.uk
www.the-icing-on-the-cake.co.uk
Provides celebration cake decorating equipment, especially for weddings.

Jane Asher Party Cakes
22–24 Cale Street
London SW3 3QU
Tel: (020) 7584 6177
Fax: (020) 7584 6179
www.jane-asher.co.uk
Range of sugarcraft equipment for sale, cake tins and wedding stands for hire.

JC Cake Supply Co.
Warehouse outlet: Unit 6
Ivanhoe Industrial Estate
Off Simsby Road
Ashby de la Zouch
Leicestershire LE65 2UU
Tel: (01530) 414554
Online catalogue: www.jccakes.com
Huge range of equipment, decorations and ingredients.

Kit Box
1 Fernlea Gardens
Easton in Gordano
Bristol BS20 0JF
Tel/Fax: (01275) 374557
Cutters, tools and templates.

Knightsbridge Bakeware Centre
Chadwell Heath Lane
Romford
Essex RN6 4NP
Tel: (020) 8590 5959
Fax: (020) 8590 7373
Email: shailesh@cakedecoration.co.uk
www.cakedecoration.co.uk
Responsible throughout the U.K. for Wilton Method Cake Decorating classes.

London Sugarart Centre
12 Selkirk Road
London SW17 0ES
Tel: (020) 8767 8558
Fax: (020) 8767 9939
Everything for the cake decorator – cake tins, cake decorating equipment and accessories.

M&B Specialised Confectioners Ltd
3a Milmead Industrial Estate
Mill Mead Road
London N17 9ND
Tel: (020) 8801 7948
Fax: (020) 8801 4663
Email: g.scott@mbsc.co.uk
www.mbsc.co.uk
Sell ready-to-roll sugarpaste in a wide variety of colours. They will even mix colours on request.

Need-A-Cake!!
47 Ravensbourne Drive
Woodley, Reading
Berkshire RG5 4LJ
Tel: (0118) 9690221
Fax: (0118) 9014228
Email: enquiries@need-a-cake.co.uk
www.need-a-cake.co.uk
Store selling cake boards, icing, edible and plastic decorations. Offer a mail-order service.

Orchard Products
51 Hallyburton Road
Hove
East Sussex BN3 7GP
Tel: 0800 9158 226
Fax: (01273) 412512
Fine quality sugarcraft cutters and tools.

Pipe Dreams
2 Bell Lane
Eton Wick
Windsor
Berkshire SL4 6JP
Tel: (01753) 865682
Tools, accessories, cake stands and tins, also courses in sugarcraft.

Renshaw Scott Ltd
229 Crown Street
Liverpool L8 7RF
Tel: (0151) 706 8200
www.renshawscott.co.uk
   or www.supercook.co.uk
Manufacturers and distributors of cake decorations and baking supplies, including the Supercook brand.

E. Russums and Sons Ltd
Edward House
Tenter Street
Rotherham
Yorkshire S60 1LB
Tel: (01709) 372345
www.russums-shop.co.uk
Sell wide range of bakeware. Shop on-line, order a catalogue or visit their showroom.

Special Occasions
39 High Street
Kirkaldy
Fife KY1 1LB
Tel: (01592) 267 635
Large selection of sugarcraft equipment.

Squire's Kitchen
International School of Cake
   Decorating and Sugarcraft
Squire's House
3 Waverley Lane
Farnham
Surrey GU9 8BB
Tel: (01252) 734309
Fax: (01252) 714714
www.squires-group.co.uk
Online shop for specialist sugarcraft
   products: www.squires-shop.co.uk
Courses in cake decoration and sugarcraft.

Sugar Daddy's
No. 1 Fishers Yard
Market Square
St Neots
Cambridgeshire PE19 2AF
Tel/Fax: (01480) 471200
Email: sugardaddys@btconnect.com
www.sugar-daddys.co.uk
Wealth of products including tins, boxes, ribbons, pillars and separators.
No mail order.

Sugar Shack
87 Burntoak Broadway
Burntoak
Middlesex HA8 5EP
Tel: 0800 5975097 (UK only) or
   (020) 8952 4260
Fax: (020) 8951 4888
Email: sales@sugarshack.co.uk
www.sugarshack.co.uk
Mail-order company specializing in cake decorating and sugarcraft supplies.

South Africa

The Baking Tin
52 Belvedere Road
Claremont
7700
Cape Town
Tel: (021) 671 6434

South Bakels
55 Section Street
Paarden Eiland
7420
Cape Town
Tel: (021) 511 1381

Confectionery Extravaganza
Shop 48, Flora Centre
Ontdekkers Road
Florida, Roodepoort
1724
Johannesburg
Tel: (011) 672 4766

South Bakels
235 Main Road
Martindale
2092
Johannesburg
Tel: (011) 673 2100

Chefs and Ices
Shop 3, Lower Level
Sandton City
Sandton
2196
Johannesburg
Tel: (011) 783 3201

Party's, Crafts and Cake Decor
Shop 4, East Rand Mall
Rietfontein Road
Boksburg
1459
Johannesburg
Tel: (011) 823 1988

Chocolate Den
Glen Dower Shopping Centre
99 Linksfield Road
Glen Dower
Edenvale
1609
Johannesburg
Tel: (011) 453 8167

The Baking Tin
Shop 108, Glenwood Village
Cnr Hunt & Moore Road
Glenwood
4001
Durban
Tel: (031) 202 2224

Jem Cutters
128 Crompton Street
Pinetown
3610
Durban
Tel: (031) 701 1431
Fax: (031) 701 0559

Bubbles Plastic
11 Cobalt Street
Border Industries
Rustenburg
0299
Tel: (014) 538 0236
Fax: (014) 538 0250

South Bakels
125 Pat Mullin Street
Bloemfontein
9301
Tel: (051) 435 7224

The Baking Tin
Rochel Road
Perridgevale
6001
Port Elizabeth
Tel: (041) 363 0271

South Bakels
41 Patterson Road
North End
6001
Port Elizabeth
Tel: (041) 484 2878

Australia

NSW
Cake Art Supplies
Kiora Mall
Shop 26 Kiora Rd
MIRANDA
NSW 2228
Tel: (02) 9540 3483

Hollywood Cake Decorations
52 Beach St
KOGARAH
NSW 2217
Tel: (02) 9587 1533

SA
The Cake Decorating Centre
36 Timwilliam St
GOODWOOD
SA 5034
Tel: (08) 8271 1171

VIC
Susie Q
Shop 4/372
Keilor Rd
NIDDRIE
VIC 3042
Tel:(03) 9379 2275

QLD
Cake and Icing Centre
651 Samford Rd
MITCHELTON
QLD 4053
Tel: (07) 3355 3443

WA
Petersen's Cake Decorations
370 Cnr South St and Stockdale Rd
OCONNOR
WA 6163
Tel: (08) 9337 9636

TAS
Gum Nut Cake and Craft Supplies
SORELL
TAS 7172
Tel: (03) 6265 1463

New Zealand

Auckland:
Chocolate Boutique
5 Mokoia Road
Birkenhead
Tel: (09) 419 2450

Decor Cakes Ltd
435 Great South Road
Otahuhu
Tel: (09) 276 6676

Golden Bridge Marketing Ltd
8 Te Kea Place
Albany
Tel: (09) 415 8777

Innovations Specialty Cookware
52 Mokoia Road
Birkenhead
Tel: (09) 480 8885

Milly's Kitchen Shop
273 Ponsonby Road
Ponsonby
Tel: (09) 376 1550

Regina Special Cake Designs
419 Dominion Road
Mt Eden
Tel: (09) 638 6363

Spotlight
(branches throughout New Zealand)
19 Link Drive
Glenfield
Tel: (09) 444 0220
www.spotlightonline.co.nz

Sugarcrafts NZ Ltd
99 Queens Road
Panmure
Tel: (09) 527 6060

Wellington:
Starline Distributors Ltd
28 Jessie Street
Wellington
Tel: (04) 385 7424

Christchurch:
Hitchon International Ltd
220 Antiqua Street
Christchurch
Tel: (03) 365 3843

Icing Specialists Equipment
Shop 6, Church Corner Mall
Riccarton
Tel: (03) 348 6828

To contact Carol Deacon, or for further information on her books, e-mail her at caroldeacon@hotmail.com or visit her website at www.caroldeacon.com.

INDEX

A

almond madeira sponge 10

B

Baby face 50–1
Baby's cradle 108–9
baking tins 8
    hiring 16, 20
    unusual shaped 9, 16
balloons, Party 69
blossom, Spring 54–5
bootees 83
bought cakes 40
bows, Christmas 102–3
Bouquet of hyacinths 52–3
broderie anglaise technique 83
buttercream 26–8
    colouring 26
    flavours 26
    flowers 43, 49, 53
    freezing 27
    frozen transfer 50–1, 54–5
    on number-shaped cake 18, 19
    pillars on 25
    piping 28
Buttercream beauty 56–7
Buttercream flowers 42–3
butterflies, Pretty 39

C

cake board, to cover 62, 93, 95
cake stands 24
candles 24
Candy house 46–7
Celebration cake 32–3
chequered sponge 13
Choc 'n' nut 138–9
chocolate: covering cake with 116
    feathers 128–9
    flowers 118
    leaves 117, 137
    melting 114
    modelling with 118
    shapes 117, 130–1
    types of 114
chocolate buttercream 26
chocolate cake 12; Quick 120–1
chocolate chip cake 132
Chocolate extravaganza 134–5
Chocolate feathers 128–9
chocolate ganache 116
chocolate madeira sponge 10
chocolate microwave cake 15
chocolate paste 118
chocolate ring, White 136–7
Chocolate shapes 130–1
chocolate truffles 118
chocolates, marzipan 123
Christening cake 82–3
Christmas bows 103–4
Christmas parcel 78–9
Christmas stars 106–7
cocoa painting 126–7
coconut madeira sponge 10
colouring: buttercream 26
    marzipan 88
    royal icing 91
    sugarpaste 63–4
combing 28, 49, 54, 58
covering a cake: with buttercream 27–8
    with chocolate 116
    with marzipan 85–7
    with royal icing 92, 94
    with sugarpaste 61
cradle, Baby's 108–9
crimping 65
cup cake, Monster 132–3
cutters for sugarpaste 65
cutting cake 8

D

decorations, instant 24, 35
dinosaur 71
doily pattern 120
dragon, Fearsome 71
dusting powder, edible 39, 57, 88

E

Easter cake 124–5
Easter teddy 125
edible dusting powder 39, 57, 88
embossed effect 65
equipment 22–3
    for piping 96
eyes 58, 75

F

fairy cakes 10, 71
Fearsome dragon 70–1
feathers, chocolate 128
figures: marzipan 125, 138
    sugarpaste 66, 80–1, 132
filling a layer cake 27
flavourings 26
flowers: buttercream 43, 49, 53
    chocolate paste 118
    Frosted 73
    frozen transfer 54–5
    Piped 110–11
    royal icing 99, 110–11
    sugarpaste 66
    Summer 48–9
    using sweets 33
fondant icing see sugarpaste
freezing: buttercream 27; see also frozen
        buttercream transfer
    chocolate cake 12
    fruit cake 14
    madeira sponge 10
Frosted flowers 72–3
frozen buttercream transfer 50–1, 54–5
fruit cake 14
    covering with marzipan 85–7
    covering with sugarpaste 61
    lining tin for 9
fruits: dipped in chocolate 117
    marzipan 88

G

gardener, Happy 80–1

H

Halloween cake, Scary 74–5
Happy gardener 80–1
heart-shaped cake 39, 76
Hearts and ribbons 76–7
house, Candy 46–7
hyacinths, Bouquet of 52–3

I

instant decorations 24, 35

L

layer cake, filling 27
layers, assembling 27
leaves: buttercream 33
    chocolate 117, 137
    paper 35
letterpress 100
letters 20–1
lining a cake tin 9

M

madeira sponge 10
marbling: buttercream 28
    sugarpaste 64, 75
marquetry 78
marzipan 84
    colouring 88
    covering cakes with 85–7
    modelling with 88
    softening 84
Marzipan chocolates 122–3
microwave cakes 15
modelling: chocolate paste 118
    marzipan 88
    sugarpaste 66, 80–1, 83
Monster cup cake 132–3

I

ers: cake 16, 18–19
    cing 98

O

orange/lemon madeira sponge 10

P

painting: cocoa 126–7
    on sugarpaste 64
parcel, Christmas 78–9
Party balloons 68–9
Piped flowers 110–11
piping: buttercream 28
    ganache 116
    royal icing 95, 98–100
piping bags 96–7, 98
piping nozzles 22, 98
pillars 24, 25
plaques 66, 83
    painting 126
portions 8
Pretty butterflies 38–9
pudding bowl cake 10
Puppet on a string 44–5

Q

quantity: of cake mixture 9, 10
    of marzipan 84
    of royal icing 90
    of sugarpaste 60
Quick chocolate cake 120–1
quilted effect 65

R

ready-to-roll icing see sugarpaste
ribbon insertion 76
ribbons 24, 35, 61, 103
rice paper 39, 57, 131, 135
royal icing 90
    colouring 91
    covering board with 93, 95
    covering cake with 92, 94
    flowers 99, 110–11
    marzipan for 86–7
    peaked 91
    pillars on 25
    piping 95, 98–100
    swirled 91
    writing with 99
runouts 100, 109, 113
    chocolate 117

S

Scary Halloween cake 74–5
scribing 99
"setting up" 28
Silver wedding cake 34–5
sizes of cake 8
snail trail 98
Snowflakes 112–13
Spring blossom 54–5
star-shaped cake 104
stars, stencilled 107
stencilling 107
stripy sponge 13
sugarpaste 60
    colouring 63–4
    covering board with 62
    covering cake with 61
    cutters for 65
    marquetry 78
    modelling 66, 80–1, 83
    on number-shaped cake 19
    pillars on 25
    roses 66
Summer flowers 48–9
sweets 36, 40, 44, 46, 50, 69, 75
swirls 28

T

Take the train 40–1
Teddy bear 36–7
templates: for buttercream 29–31
    for chocolate 119
    for royal icing 101
    for sugarpaste 67
train, Take the 40
troubleshooting 15
twisted strands 65

V

vanilla microwave cake 15

W

Wedding star 104–5
White chocolate ring 136–7
Who's looking at you? 58–9
woodgrain effect 63
writing with royal icing 99